CONTENTS

ACKNOWLEDGEMENTS

I am grateful to the International Maritime Organization (IMO) for permission to reprint the International Regulations for Preventing Collisions at Sea and to the Marine Directorate of the Department of Transport for their permission to re-produce the diagram of the Dover Strait Traffic Separation Scheme.

I am also indebted to many professional seamen and pleasure-craft skippers for spending time discussing various aspects of the rules and giving their views on how best pleasure and commercial craft can share the waters of the world. Their input forms a major part of much of what is fundamental to its objectives. Although some of their words are quoted, much of what has been set out as comment and discussion on the rules themselves has been based upon their thoughts and ideas.

To thank all of these people personally would result in a very long list. While all deserve a mention, the following took time from already hectic schedules to help: Captains Chris Sample and Ian Tomkins of P. & O. Cruises who also let me travel on the bridge of the cruise ship *Sea Princess*; Captains Andy Hill and Geoff Hepple of P. & O. Bulk Carriers for giving me an insight into the world of the big bulk cargo ships; the pilots who safely conduct a real cross-section of commercial vessels into and out of the Solent; Captain Neil Varney of British Channel Island Ferries' MV *Rozel* and Captain John Francis of Red Funnel's MV *Norris Castle* for letting me see at first hand the problems and requirements that they and their officers face when navigating in areas most popular with pleasure craft; Captain John Lloyd of Hoverspeed for showing me the complexities and special needs of this high-speed form of travel; Southampton Harbour Master Captain M. J. Ridge, his assistant, Captain K. J. Styles and the crews of the launch *Millbrook* with whom I spent some time on patrol; Captain David James, Chief Surveyor, Marine Division of the Department of Transport and HM Coast-guard Station Officer Eric Musson at the Channel Navigation Information Service at Langdon Battery, Dover, who between them showed just how important is the task of observing and administering the Traffic Separation Scheme and the Channel Navigation Information Service for the Dover Strait; and last but not least my friend and colleague Mik Chinery, who through his teaching has given many hundreds of students the confidence and judgement needed to make the fullest and safest use of their own small boats.

PREFACE

Taking your own small boat into tidal waters inhabited by commercial ships and professional mariners for the first time is an occasion for greatly mixed emotions. Pride, fear and nervous but pleasurable anticipation are just a few. You almost become a child again, beguiled and bewitched by the unwritten promises of the greatest temptress of all time – the sea herself.

The sea has its own set of rules and has many moods. In time you will learn to understand and even anticipate these moods. Above all you will learn that the sea must be respected. If that respect is tinged with a little fear it will be no bad thing. Through understanding will come enjoyment and through respect will come a sense of balanced judgement for what is safe and what is not.

But safety at sea today needs more than an understanding of the sea itself; it needs more than the traditional skills of boat handling and an understanding of winds and tides. The sea and the inlets and creeks, canals and waterways that stem from it or flow to it are no longer the lonely places beloved of the Ancient Mariner. The sea today is a busy place. To enjoy it and stay safe, every skipper whatever his or her nationality, in charge of an ocean liner or a tramp steamer, a yacht or a motor cruiser or any type of craft, must know, understand and abide by one set of rules.

Based upon a set of recommendations prepared in 1840, the International Regulations for Preventing Collisions at Sea form the mariner's Highway Code and must be known and understood by everyone that may ever be in charge of a vessel of any size navigating the tidal waters of the world. Since they were originally drafted in 1840, traffic at sea and around the coasts of the world has increased enormously. New technology and modern power plants have created huge differences in the size and speed of vessels. There has also been a massive increase in the numbers of pleasure craft of all kinds and sizes both around the coasts and traversing the oceans.

New technology has also brought many benefits to seafarers especially in the fields of navigation and observation with Decca, Loran, GPS, radar and the like. But these benefits have also introduced new levels of danger. Navigation can now be so precise that vessels travelling between the same points face the very real danger of running into each other because they are on precisely the same tracks.

Commercial pressures have created the need for greater speed as shippers require guaranteed delivery times for their goods. Rigid schedules are also the norm for the ferry services that run in European waters and elsewhere. Timetables are tight and minor diversions from pre-planned courses can mean loss of profits.

The International Regulations for

PREFACE

Preventing Collisions at Sea, as we know them today, have been created and refined to ensure that every person in charge of a vessel, regardless of size or type, knows and understands what is required of him or her and what may be expected of others.

Rules and regulations of course do not prevent collisions – people do, and the judgement of any given situation can vary from person to person. Making judgements is a major part of any activity at sea. There are no white lines, traffic lights or signs that dictate right of way, and speed and direction are not instantly controllable by a pedal or a wheel. The matter of individual judgement therefore assumes critical importance. Much of what is contained within the Regulations is designed to ensure that judgements can be based upon a common set of principles thus creating the minimum leeway for error. Having said that, no two situations will ever be exactly the same so there can be no specifics. But this is why so many people take to the sea for pleasure. They do not want to be bound by white lines and the route of any given road. The freedom of the seas will always be there and taking time to understand the Regulations and act accordingly will help to ensure a real enjoyment of that freedom.

In recent years there has been a massive increase in the numbers of large and small pleasure craft on the waters of the world. These range from the multi-million-pound playthings of the exceptionally wealthy to the sailing or power-driven boats and cruisers of the man and woman next door. The wealthy employ trained and qualified professional skippers and crew to man their craft. It is for the others, the man and woman next door who take to the waters of the world in charge of their own small boats, that this book has been written.

At the time of writing there is no legal requirement in the United Kingdom for pleasure-boat owners or skippers to pass any form of test of competency before taking to the water. Many in fact do study for and take the various levels of certificates laid down and prepared by the Royal Yachting Association. All of these require a good knowledge and understanding of the content and spirit of the International Regulations for Preventing Collisions at Sea. Whether tests of competency become mandatory or not, anyone in charge of a boat of any size or type will make life safer for themselves and everybody else upon the water by taking time to study the requirements placed upon them by these 'rules of the road'.

This book is designed to help newcomers to the pleasures of boating to understand why the rules say what they do. It is designed to help create an awareness of the needs and problems faced by those in charge of different kinds of vessels with which the reader may be unfamiliar.

In preparing this book I have assumed that the reader has a basic knowledge of seamanship and its associated terms and language. Because not all power boat people understand the principles of sailing, and because not all sailors appreciate the factors governing the activities of power boats, I have included passages to help each understand the other.

I make no apologies for repetition within these pages. Several rules may be appropriate to any one situation and several different situations may require similar considerations. If repetition helps get the message home in a manner that ensures a quick and correct response then it must surely be justified.

Gavin Davies

INTRODUCTION

How the rules have evolved

Just over 100 years ago the first International Maritime Conference was held in Washington to consider creating a set of regulations, designed to prevent collisions at sea, that would be approved and enforced by international agreement. Rules of one sort or another had been in existence for 200 or 300 years before this, but they were not backed up by any form of statutory force until the advent of what we now call the International Regulations for Preventing Collisions at Sea.

The 1889 Washington conference based its deliberations on a set of rules that had been drawn up in 1840 by the Corporation of Trinity House in London and which had been approved by the British Parliament in 1846. Trinity House was incorporated in 1514 as an association for piloting ships, and since then it has been intimately involved in a wide range of matters involved in British maritime navigation.

Even during those early years between 1840 and 1889 additions and alterations had to be made to the rules drafted by Trinity House to take into account the emergence of steam and more modern forms of power-driven vessels, and the consequent variations in the size, speed and manoeuvrability of waterborne traffic. It is worth remembering that for many years most sailing vessels could only travel when the wind blew from behind. Any form of manoeuvre on a large, fully rigged ship could take some time and a fair amount of sea room, but there was not the rush or the crush that exists today and skippers made way for each other as a matter of course.

The start of the nineteenth century saw the real emergence of power-driven vessels. Their numbers and size increased rapidly as merchants of the world realized how increased speed and reliability could help them bring more products to a wider range of markets. Ports were built to speed up loading and unloading procedures where anchorages and barges had previously sufficed, and as the ships grew bigger so did the need to mark and dredge the channels to and from the ports.

While the ports grew, so did the ancillary traffic. Pilot boats, tugs, barges, and coal, fuel and supply boats were designed and built to carry out their specific tasks. Power and sail boats met, and were often commanded by captains from different parts of the world. The increase in traffic, collisions and incidents soon brought a realization that there was a need for a set of rules that could be understood by all and which would take account of the abilities and priorities of the now huge range of seagoing traffic.

The regulations that had been discussed and agreed to at the Washington conference in 1889 were brought into force by

INTRODUCTION

Britain, the United States and a number of other countries in 1897. A further conference in Brussels in 1910 brought minor changes and amendments to those regulations and, very importantly, included the approval and enforcement by more countries.

The 1910 regulations, with amendments, remained in force until 1954 when wide-ranging changes were made to cover the quickening pace of change and development in the maritime world. A further revision of these regulations was undertaken in 1960 at the International Conference on Safety of Life at Sea, convened in London by the Inter-governmental Maritime Consultative Organization (IMCO).

The most recent major revisions were agreed to in 1972 at a conference in London, hosted by IMCO and attended by delegations, representatives and observers from fifty-two countries and many governmental and non-governmental organizations. Further detailed changes were agreed at the fifteenth assembly of the International Maritime Organization in November 1987 and these came into force in November 1989.

As times and technology change so will the rules, but the time and effort expended by the governments of the world to ensure that there is one set of rules that can and should be followed by everyone serves to highlight their importance to every seafarer.

The International Regulations for Preventing Collisions at Sea, 1972, sometimes called the Colregs, or rules of the road, are divided into five sections containing thirty-eight specifically numbered rules. They also include four annexes that cover technical aspects of lights, shapes and sound signals as well as distress signals and additional signals for vessels fishing in close proximity.

In this book I go through the rules in their proper order with comment and discussion on each rule and group of rules. The ultimate objective is to help the reader to balance the dictates of the regulations with the actualities of situations that may be encountered at sea.

Few small-boat skippers have actual experience of the needs and problems facing their counterparts in big ships – those who earn their living in the multitude of vessels carrying cargo, passengers or both in the oceans, seas and rivers of the world. I have tried to give an insight into this other side of the seagoing coin with comments from a number of these professional seamen, many of whom have small boats themselves. Hopefully this will help the reader to understand more fully why many of the rules stipulate the actions they do. This should also help the novice to judge what the best action may be in any given situation by creating a better understanding of the factors that may affect others as well as himself or herself.

Much of what is discussed in this book relates directly to the practice of good seamanship and the ideas and advice given may not always appear to have a specific relationship with the rules as such. But the practice of good seamanship on any vessel will always render her and her crew better able to take action quickly and efficiently to follow the requirements of the rules.

1
GENERAL RULES

The first three rules form a preface that clearly identifies where and by whom the regulations as a whole must be followed and outlines some of the circumstances that may give rise to departures from them. Here also we find the basic definitions of some of the words and phrases that are used throughout.

Rule 1

APPLICATION

(a)   These Rules shall apply to all vessels upon the high seas and in all waters connected therewith navigable by sea-going vessels.

(b)   Nothing in these Rules shall interfere with the operation of special rules made by an appropriate authority for roadsteads, harbours, rivers, lakes or inland water-ways connected with the high seas and navigable by seagoing vessels. Such special rules shall conform as closely as possible to these Rules.

(c)   Nothing in these Rules shall interfere with the operation of any special rules made by the Government of any State with respect to additional station or signal lights, shapes or whistle signals for ships of war and vessels proceeding under convoy, or with respect to additional station or signal lights or shapes for fishing vessels engaged in fishing as a fleet. These additional station or signal lights, shapes or whistle signals shall, so far as possible, be such that they cannot be mistaken for any light, shape or signal authorized elsewhere under these Rules.

(d)   Traffic separation schemes may be adopted by the Organization for the purpose of these Rules.

(e)   Whenever the Government concerned shall have determined that a vessel of special construction or purpose cannot comply fully with the provisions of any of these Rules with respect to the number, position, range or arc of visibility of lights or shapes, as well as to the disposition and characteristics of sound-signalling appliances, such vessel shall comply with such other provisions in regard to the number, position, range or arc of visibility of lights or shapes, as well as to the disposition and characteristics of sound-signalling appliances, as her Government shall have determined to be the closest possible compliance with these Rules in respect of that vessel.

Rule 2

RESPONSIBILITY

(a)   Nothing in these Rules shall exonerate any vessel, or the owner, master or crew thereof, from the consequences of any neglect to comply with these Rules or of the neglect of any precaution which may be required by the ordinary practice of seamen, or by the special circumstances of the case.

Size and speed make no difference to the need to comply with every aspect of the rules.

(b) In construing and complying with these Rules due regard shall be had to all dangers of navigation and collision and to any special circumstances, including the limitations of the vessels involved, which may make a departure from these Rules necessary to avoid immediate danger.

Rule 3

GENERAL DEFINITIONS

For the purpose of these Rules, except where the context otherwise requires:

(a) The word 'vessel' includes every description of water craft, including non-displacement craft and seaplanes, used or capable of being used as a means of transportation on water.

(b) The term 'power-driven vessel' means any vessel propelled by machinery.

(c) The term 'sailing vessel' means any vessel under sail provided that propelling machinery, if fitted, is not being used.

(d) The term 'vessel engaged in fishing' means any vessel fishing with nets, lines, trawls or other fishing apparatus which restrict manoeuvrability, but does not include a vessel fishing with trolling lines or other fishing apparatus which do not restrict manoeuvrability.

(e) The word 'seaplane' includes any aircraft designed to manoeuvre on the water.

(f) The term 'vessel not under command' means a vessel which through some exceptional circumstance is unable to manoeuvre as required by these Rules and is therefore unable to keep out of the way of another vessel.

(g) The term 'vessel restricted in her ability to manoeuvre' means a vessel which from the nature of her work is restricted in her ability to manoeuvre as required by these Rules and is therefore unable to keep out of the way of another vessel. The term 'vessels restricted in their ability to manoeuvre' shall include but not be limited to:

(i) a vessel engaged in laying, servicing or picking up a navigation mark, submarine cable or pipeline;

(ii) a vessel engaged in dredging, surveying or underwater operations;

(iii) a vessel engaged in replenishment or transferring persons, provisions or cargo while under way;

(iv) a vessel engaged in the launching or recovery of aircraft;

(v) a vessel engaged in mine clearance operations;

(vi) a vessel engaged in a towing operation such as severely restricts the towing vessel and her tow in their ability to deviate from their course.

(h) The term 'vessel constrained by her draught' means a power-driven vessel which, because of her draught in relation to the available depth and width of navigable water, is severely restricted in her ability to deviate from the course she is following.

(i) The word 'under way' means that a vessel is not at anchor, or made fast to the shore, or aground.

(j) The words 'length' and 'breadth' of a vessel mean her length overall and greatest breadth.

(k) Vessels shall be deemed to be in sight of one another only when one can be observed visually from the other.

(l) The term 'restricted visibility' means any condition in which visibility is restricted by fog, mist, falling snow, heavy rainstorms, sandstorms or any other similar causes.

Discussion on Rules 1, 2 and 3

RULE 1

The first lines of Rule 1 clearly illustrate the international nature of the rules. 'All vessels' and 'all waters' leaves little room for doubt as to where and to whom they are applicable. This rule also indicates that the mariner may come across special local rules that supersede some of the regulations. These special local rules may be made by governments or local authorities to cover specific areas of water. They may also relate to naval or fishing vessels that are unable to comply fully with the regulations concerning the display of lights, shapes and other specific equipment because of their construction or some other particular and accepted reason.

This highlights the importance of proper planning before venturing into unfamiliar waters. Details of special regulations can usually be found in pilot books covering the areas to be visited. They are also covered in the Admiralty Sailing Directions although these are only updated every eighteen months.

For the most part, special signals set by local authorities or individual governments will be to do with entering and leaving harbours or narrow waterways, or they may cover signals to be given by vessels manoeuvring within their limits.

It is doubtful that you will encounter ships travelling in convoy as discussed in Rule 1(c) but you may well encounter fishing fleets. On both counts, however, the simplest answer is to recognize them for what they are – a major hazard – and keep well clear.

Traffic separation schemes play an increasing role in ensuring the safety of both commercial and leisure shipping in the world today and you will find this subject discussed in detail with Rule 10 (*see* pages 50–58).

Warships can face and pose particular problems. Some are constructed in such a manner that they are not able to show the lights and shapes as they are prescribed within the context of these rules. Submarines for example will carry their lights much lower than would be expected for vessels of their size. This may make them appear further away than they really are. Other naval vessels may carry lights in positions that make it difficult to readily identify what aspect they are presenting to the observer.

However, whatever the circumstance, any and all vessels are required to keep their lights as closely as possible in accord with those prescribed for vessels of their type and size. So if you see something out of the ordinary, take a good look but do not assume anything until every possibility has been explored.

RULE 2

Rule 2 highlights the fact that there will often be situations where adherence to the letter of the rules may not be appropriate. Indeed, saying that you acted according to the rules may well not help, should you be involved in a collision where other circumstances should have been taken into consideration.

It is the responsibility of the skipper, officer of the watch or whoever is in charge of a vessel at the time to assess each situation with regard to what the rules say, what good seamanship dictates and having regard to any other factors that may have to be taken into account. This must include the proximity of other vessels, navigational hazards such as shoals or rocks plus a sensible assessment of the

The driver of the rigid hull inflatable must be equally aware of the needs of the rules as the skippers of the sailing yacht and the luxury cruiser.

probable abilities of the other vessels involved. A sailing boat under power heading up a narrow channel may have to stay close to the middle of the channel because of her draft. Similarly a power boat running into a narrow channel with the wind and sea behind her may have to travel faster than usual in order to maintain steerage way. In either case it would be easy to criticize their skippers, but in truth neither has an option. People prevent collisions through a balanced judgement of the facts they see before them. If, following a judgement of the facts, a departure from the rules is deemed necessary to avoid danger then that is the course that must be taken.

It must always be remembered that the regulations themselves do not give right of way to any vessel. Right of way is only given by one vessel altering her course or speed for another. Everyone is responsible for taking action to avoid the risk of collision. The regulations as a whole have been created to ensure that actions taken to avoid collision will follow a predictable pattern except where special circumstances demand otherwise. Essentially they are a code of conduct that is common to all vessels regardless of size, speed, motive power or nationality.

RULE 3

Rule 3 defines precisely a number of the words and phrases that are used within the context of the rules. Subsection (c) clearly states that the term 'sailing vessel' applies only to a vessel that is at the time relying solely on the wind to move her through the water. Subsection (i) means that if a vessel is not connected to the ground or the shore then she is 'under way' even if she is making no way through the water.

The Big Ships

Common sense dictates that it is much easier for a small craft to keep out of the way of a big ship anywhere other than in the open sea. Out at sea with the benefit of radar the big ship may see the small craft first and make an alteration to its course before she has appeared over the horizon.

A course alteration for a small craft means putting the wheel or tiller over and maybe making some adjustments to the set of the sails, but for a big ship the procedure is much more complex. It takes longer for the action of the rudder to influence the direction of the ship and she will need much more sea room for an equivalent degree of change to her course. In some instances engine movements may take some time to happen if the vessel has been steaming at full speed. On some ships there is a distinct delay between going ahead and going astern because of the way the propellers are linked to the gearboxes or engines.

Many of the most recent additions and amendments to the rules have been made to take account of the problems and needs of the big ships without losing sight in any way of the rights and requirements of small craft. One of the most recently introduced phrases that directly reflects the needs of the big ships is the requirement ' . . . shall not impede the safe passage of . . . ' as used in Rules 9, 10 and 18.

A missed tide, a delayed departure or the need for a major course alteration in a small craft may mean that the cat gets fed late when you do eventually get home. The same problems for a big ship may cost its owners many thousands of pounds in lost revenues. The big-ship captain is expected to keep to strict schedules

QEII and high-speed catamaran – to be kept well clear of.

whether he is in charge of a passenger liner with tours and facilities for his passengers pre-booked at various ports, or in command of a bulk carrier where delay may mean a missed berth, late delivery and poorer prices for the cargo.

To help them keep to their schedules, most commercial vessels are designed to operate at a specific speed through virtually any sea condition. They also have the very latest navigation and communications equipment to give them advance warning of really bad weather and the ability to choose the best route to avoid it. But none of the equipment they carry can help them avoid close-quarter situations in enclosed or restricted waters that may be caused by other vessels, whether they be large or small.

Few small-craft skippers actually navigate within enclosed or restricted waters. They mostly rely on their knowledge of the area, or buoy hop using basic pilotage techniques. This is not so with the big ships. In inshore waters they sail on very precisely calculated courses at specific speeds. They will have a local pilot on board who has intimate knowledge of the waters they are in and who will also be aware of any temporary navigational problems that may exist. But of course each large vessel has different characteristics and many companies with big ships on regular runs will have selected pilots at their regular ports whom they use on a regular basis. This way the pilots get to know the individual ships, their captains and their officers, as well as the problems

Everything looks very small from the bridge of the *Sea Princess*.

and capabilities of the ships themselves.

Chris Sample is one of the senior captains in the P. & O. fleet and has commanded several of the cruise liners that the company operates. He believes that few small-boat skippers actually realize that big ships must stick to very specific tracks and courses in narrow channels. He says:

From the moment one of our ships leaves its berth the officer of the watch will be on the radar checking that it does not stray from the planned ground track. He will tell the captain or the pilot if the ship should wander by even a few metres. The captain or the pilot will then give the necessary orders to the helmsman to regain the proper track. What you have to remember is that these ships, although not officially classified as vessels constrained by their draft, do fall within this category when they are in narrow channels. They may

have just one or two cables' clearance each side before they will be on the putty, and maybe less than this under some conditions. So while they may be able to slow down or stop, which leaves them at the mercy of wind or tide, they can actually do very little in the way of course alterations without a real risk of running aground.

Apart from the captain and the pilot, a number of other officers and seamen will be on the bridge of a P. & O. cruise liner like the *Sea Princess* when she leaves or enters port. The deputy captain, the chief officer, two junior officers, a helmsman, a lookout and a messenger all have parts to play in ensuring the safe passage of this 25,100 tonne (27,670 ton) ship with her crew of 400 and nearly 900 passengers. Once at sea and clear of busy shipping lanes this number will be reduced to perhaps three, but it is never less.

Once clear of the berth it is the pilot who gives the orders for course and speed changes, although the captain is still in command. Before departure the pilot will have made the captain aware of any specific problems that may exist in the area and they will have agreed how these problems will be dealt with. These could relate to a speed restriction in the area of a recent wreck or the need to pass another vessel at a specific point in the channel. Once clear of her berth and on line to move down channel she will let go her tugs' lines (unless there is a high wind) and then gather way slowly using bursts of power from the engines that will take her up to her minimum manoeuvring speed of about 7.5 knots. Once clear of the narrowest parts of the channel she will work up to about 16 knots before slowing down again to let the pilot off.

Cruising speeds for different ships vary as do their abilities to stop and turn. In a calm sea with less than 10 knots of wind, no current and plenty of water under her keel, the *Sea Princess* for example can make a crash stop from full speed in just under three-and-a-half minutes. In the process she will cover about half a mile and this is also the diameter of the circle she could turn with the wheel hard over at full speed. But these distances and times only relate to full emergency procedures undertaken in ideal conditions with a calm sea and a wind of less than 10 knots.

Bigger ships will need more space and time for similar manoeuvres and some may need slightly less. A 250,000 tonne supertanker would obviously need much more space and time than the *Sea Princess*

This is a view you should never have of a large vessel leaving its berth. You should stay well clear.

Well laid out control and communication systems on the bridge of the 110,000-tonne bulk carrier *Pytchley*.

to stop or turn, but a naval frigate that is designed to be manoeuvrable at speed will make rings round or inside both of them.

Bulk carriers and container ships which have their bridge structures set well aft or whose forward view is restricted by several levels of containers on the foredeck will have a blind area dead ahead and for some distance – up to 0.3–0.5 mile (0.5–0.8km) – on each side of the bows. A small craft cutting close ahead will therefore be lost to view for some time in this area which will also be blind to radar. Small craft must assume that they can not be seen if they themselves can not see the forward windows of the other vessel's bridge. They should not be this close anyway.

When big ships are approaching or leaving an anchorage they will be travelling at well below their manoeuvrable speeds just before letting go or leaving. Small craft should stay clear of areas that are commonly used as commercial anchorages if they see ships approaching or leaving them. The same is true of the areas where they pick up and drop their pilots. Before picking up or dropping a pilot the ship will turn on to a course and slow down to a speed that has been selected to suit the weather conditions and the abilities of the pilot

Captain Geoff Hepple checks anchor bearings
from the bridge wing of the *Pytchley*.

craft. This may not be dead slow, but once the pilot has left the bridge to disembark, the ship will hold her course and speed while the pilot boat comes alongside and collects or delivers the pilot. So, once again small craft should stay clear while this manoeuvre is under way. Once the pilot boat has cleared away, the ship may well make a marked alteration of course as she might have altered to make a lee for the pilot boat to come alongside.

Both the rules and common sense dictate that in general terms small craft should keep clear of big ones in restricted waters. When reading the rules it is worth bearing in mind the restrictions faced by the big ships while accepting that they do not have a general mandate to assume that small craft must keep out of their way at all times.

SUMMARY OF RULES 1–3

- Having read this first part of the rules you should now understand to whom they refer and where they apply.

- You should be aware that you may find different or additional rules in certain areas or applied to certain types or groups of vessels, and you should know where you will find details of these variations.

- You should have a clear understanding of the precise meanings of the most important words and phrases as they are used within the context of the rules.

- You should be fully aware of the responsibilities of those in charge of any vessel.

- Most importantly, you must understand that, as well as complying with the requirements of the rules, you and every other person in charge of a vessel of any size are required to observe the practice of good seamanship at all times.

2

STEERING AND SAILING RULES

The steering and sailing rules are divided into three separate subsections.

Section I deals with the general behaviour and conduct of vessels in any condition of visibility whether they are in sight of each other or not. It also covers the very specific requirements of vessels using and crossing traffic separation schemes.

Section II covers the conduct of vessels that are in sight of each other and is arguably the most important section for the small-boat skipper to know and understand. It details actions that should be taken in specific situations and denotes responsibilities.

Section III covers the conduct of vessels in restricted visibility and outlines some of the precautions that should be taken to minimize the chances of close-quarters situations developing.

Section I – Conduct of vessels in any condition of visibility

Rule 4

APPLICATION
Rules in this section apply in any condition of visibility.

Rule 5

LOOKOUT
Every vessel shall at all times maintain a proper lookout by sight and hearing as well as by all available means appropriate in the prevailing circumstances and conditions so as to make a full appraisal of the situation and of the risk of collision.

Discussion on Rules 4 and 5

RULE 4
Rule 4 simply restates that rules in Section I (Rules 4 to 10) apply in *any* condition of visibility.

RULE 5
Without doubt, the single most important activity on any vessel in any weather or sea condition is that of keeping a good look-out. Rule 5 states: 'Every vessel shall *at all times* [author's stress] maintain a proper lookout'. There are no exceptions to this. At all times means at all times, and not every five minutes or so. The rule also says that the lookout should be maintained 'by all available means'. This does not mean sitting in the cabin with your head in the radar, unless you also have someone in the cockpit using the best means available – namely the eyes.

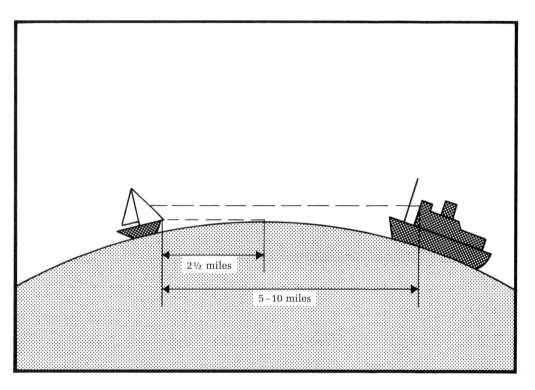

Depending on the actual height of eye of the observers on the bridge of the big ship, or in the cockpit or on the flying bridge of the sailing or motor yacht, horizon distances will vary between 2.5 miles (4km) from 2m (6ft) above the waterline to about 10 miles (16km) from 23m (75ft) up.

On a small boat keeping a good lookout is even more critical than on a large vessel because of the speed with which close-quarters situations can develop. This is because of the limited range of vision that one has from just a few feet above the surface of the sea. For the average small-boat sailor in a reasonably calm sea, a height of eye of 2m (6ft) will give a visible horizon distance of just under 3 miles (5km). If the sea is in any way rough this distance can decrease to a few hundred yards with just an occasional glimpse of beyond from the tops of the waves. At 24 knots a fast tanker or container ship would cover this distance in under eight minutes. The flying bridge of a motor cruiser may give a horizon range of about 5 miles (8km), but that is still not very far when meeting the big, fast, cargo boats of today.

It is therefore essential that a good look-out be kept by day and by night. By day the main problem for the sailing crew is usually seeing under or round the foresail and indeed to leeward of the main if the boat is close hauled and heeled over. Where crew are available one should be positioned on the lower or lee side of the cockpit with the specific task of looking out over the helmsman's blind spots. If short-handed, then the boat must be

Loaded up like this, the view of the water ahead is restricted for the bridge crew of this container ship. Sharing the channel with it is not good sense.

swung off course every so often to allow the helmsman to scan these areas.

Although Rule 13 states that it is the duty of the overtaking vessel to keep clear, do not forget to look astern. An overtaking vessel might not have seen you or it could be a vessel that is for some reason restricted in its ability to manoeuvre.

It is also a fact that there is a cone of silence directly in front of any power-driven vessel from where her engines will not be heard. Many yacht cockpits are totally surrounded by dodgers which tend to shield the occupants from external sounds as well as from wind and spray. A conscious effort must be made to look up

and over them. From an inside steering position in either a motor-sailer or a motor boat, the problem is even more acute as visibility will also be restricted by parts of the boat itself.

A good lookout will alternate between using his eyes and scanning the horizon with binoculars. Many people will pick out objects with the naked eye before they see them for the first time using binoculars. In bad weather binoculars are difficult to hold steady and will not give a good image if they get covered in spray. An important tip here: do not buy the most powerful binoculars you can find; buy the best pair of 7 × 50s that you can afford.

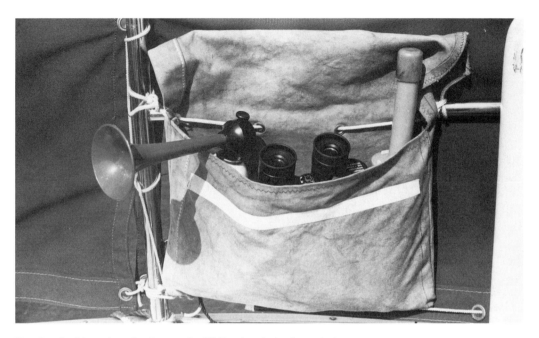

Keeping the binoculars, fog-horn and a lifeline handy in the cockpit.

The binoculars should always be ready to hand so that anything sighted can quickly be identified and a decision made as to whether there is a need to take some form of action. A good hand-bearing compass should also be handy so that the possibility of collision can be checked with a series of bearings as quickly as possible.

At night the same requirements prevail. It is critically important that everyone understands the need to conserve night vision. It takes about fifteen minutes for the eye to adjust to darkness after being exposed to white light, and for this reason red lights, which do not damage night vision, should be used at the chart table. Crew coming into the cockpit should also take care to extinguish any cabin lights that may dazzle those on watch. Those coming on watch should also be given

time to adjust their eyes before the old watch goes below.

When approaching a harbour at night it may be necessary to use a hand-held spotlight to find a mooring buoy or check berth numbers on pontoons. If this is necessary care must be taken not to shine it anywhere near the faces of the helmsmen or crew of other boats in the vicinity.

In fog a lookout should be posted in the bows where not only eyes but also ears can be brought to bear with the minimum of distraction. In fog things happen much more quickly so a few extra seconds of warning can be critically important. This will be discussed further with Rule 19.

Rule 5 also states that the lookout should be kept by 'all available means'. So, if you have radar use it. But radar must be thought of as secondary to the basic eye work. It must not be relied upon to the

No reflectors but scanners mounted as high as possible on these power cruisers.

exclusion of all else. If you have radar it is important that you understand what it is telling you. It is a specialized subject and we will not dwell on it here except to say that used properly by a skilled operator a good radar set can be of great help in avoiding close-quarters situations. On the other hand, radar-assisted collisions do happen – often in poor weather when it is much more pleasant to stay inside the cabin and watch the screen than sit outside and dodge the rain or spray.

Many power boats and motor-sailers have enclosed steering positions that keep the elements at bay. But sometimes this is at the expense of good all-round visibility. Although forward vision is generally fairly good there can be extensive blind areas on the quarters which the lookout

must cover by moving himself or the vessel.

Although not a requirement within the rules, it helps others to spot you if you have a good quality radar reflector mounted as high as possible. If it is the octahedral type do make sure that it is hoisted in the correct 'rain catching' position.

Rule 6

SAFE SPEED

Every vessel shall at all times proceed at a safe speed so that she can take proper and effective action to avoid collision and be stopped within a distance appropriate to the prevailing circumstances and conditions.

This will give only an intermittent echo when the boat rolls as it is mounted incorrectly.

The nearest yacht has a good set-up with both radar and a good modern reflector mounted at a good height.

In determining a safe speed the following factors shall be among those taken into account:

(a) By all vessels:
(i) the state of visibility;
(ii) the traffic density including concentrations of fishing vessels or any other vessels;
(iii) the manoeuvrability of the vessel with special reference to stopping distance and turning ability in the prevailing conditions;
(iv) at night the presence of background light such as from shore lights or from back scatter of her own lights;
(v) the state of wind, sea and current, and the proximity of navigational hazards;
(vi) the draught in relation to the available depth of water.

(b) Additionally, by vessels with operational radar:

(i) the characteristics, efficiency and limitations of the radar equipment;

(ii) any constraints imposed by the radar range scale in use;

(iii) the effect on radar detection of the sea state, weather and other sources of interference;

(iv) the possibility that small vessels, ice and other floating objects many not be detected by radar at an adequate range;

(v) the number, location and movement of vessels detected by radar;

(vi) the more exact assessment of the visibility that may be possible when radar is used to determine the range of vessels or other objects in the vicinity.

Discussion on Rule 6

What is a safe speed at sea? This depends upon a multiplicity of factors including those outlined in section (a) of Rule 6. The first two points create obvious limitations. Poor visibility and high traffic density must mean that vessels should travel at speeds slower than they would in clear weather and empty waters. How much slower will depend upon the factors in the third part of section (a), namely the manoeuvrability and stopping distance of the individual vessel.

These factors themselves will also be influenced by the prevailing weather conditions and the proximity of land or other navigational hazards. Night and poor visibility present a special set of problems, but by day and in good conditions there is a need to understand the capabilities of the other vessels (both large and small) that are seen around your craft.

At sea in clear waters – and this includes areas within the shipping lanes of the English Channel – the larger commercial cargo and passenger vessels cruise at speeds of between 15 and 25 knots. From these speeds a crash stop for them could take anything from one to several miles depending upon the state of readiness of the engines, how deeply laden they may be and any number of other factors. Turning circles might be as tight as half a mile under ideal conditions, but in other situations they could be considerably more. Whatever the case, it is not worth finding out what their abilities are if you are in a thirty-footer and they are carrying up to 250,000 tonnes of cargo.

Probably the fastest commercial craft you will ever meet will be the hovercraft or high-speed catamarans that provide the cross-Channel ferry services. The big hovercraft can and do travel at speeds of up to 65 knots – that is 75mph. Because they travel so fast, and often travel with a drift angle of up to 30 degrees it is very difficult, if not impossible, for the observer to work out their actual direction of travel, so they themselves keep out of everybody's way.

Speed is a problem for the small-boat skipper in terms of the time taken to see and be seen, to make decisions and then to act accordingly. A sailing boat travelling at 6 knots meeting a commercial vessel travelling at 24 knots with 5 miles (8km) between them will come together in just ten minutes. At a distance of 5 miles (8km) it will take the yachtsman some time to identify the size and approximate heading of the other vessel in good weather. That is always assuming that he is actually able to see the other vessel at that distance. In poor weather, which will affect him much

Do not get in his way but at the same time do not alter course in front of him. High-speed hovercraft tend to go around everyone else.

more so than it will the big ship, the yachtsman may well not see the other until it is just a couple of miles off. This leaves very little time to make decisions and take action, but again it highlights the critical importance of keeping a good lookout.

Most, if not all, big ships today have sophisticated radar systems. However, it must be remembered that in anything over about force 5, sea conditions are liable to be such that it may be difficult for them to pick out the echo from a small boat amongst the wave clutter on a radar screen. In these same conditions, it may be equally difficult to see a small vessel visually, especially if she has a white painted hull and is viewed against a background of white wave tops.

In small boats, speed, or the lack of it can be a major factor in the well-being and therefore the attentiveness of the crew. A power boat in anything over force 4

travelling at a displacement speed of about eight or nine knots will give a very uncomfortable ride to her crew and her very motion will make the keeping of an efficient lookout extremely difficult. The skipper who knows his boat may be able to increase speed to say 15 knots when the boat will sit more comfortably and probably be easier to handle.

A sailing yacht beating hard at maybe six or seven knots into a force 4 wind with all sails set and well heeled over will create the problems of visibility that we discussed under Rule 5. With a good crew and proper lookouts this need not be a problem but in congested waters it would be seamanlike to ease the main a little, bring the boat more upright and/or set a smaller jib with a higher cut clew that obscures as little as possible from the helmsman's view.

In a following sea many power boats are

more difficult to handle than sailing yachts, especially at slow speeds. This is because few of them have anything resembling a keel to hold them in a straight line. So if you are in a sailing boat and are overtaken by a power boat in a narrowish channel with wind and sea behind you, try to understand that he may well be travelling as slowly as he dares under the circumstances.

A sailing yacht rarely travels fast enough for her speed alone to be a major factor in contributing to a collision. However, this is not true of the smaller racing dinghies, catamarans and sailboards, all of whom are equally governed by the collision regulations. Many of these are capable of achieving considerably higher speeds than the average cruising or racing yacht. A GP 14 or International 470 powering through an anchorage and across a narrow channel on a broad reach with spinnaker flying and both crew out on trapeze may be exhilarating to watch. It

could also have all the makings of a disaster should they get caught by a puff and capsize in the channel in the path of something big and unmanoeuvrable. Similarly, small ski-boats with large outboards and the new wetbikes are often seen travelling at dangerously high speeds in close proximity to other boats. Rule 6 and all of the other rules apply equally to them as they do to a 250,000 tonne supertanker. There is no discrimination with regard to the size of vessel to which the rules apply. It is worth repeating that part of Rule 1 which states: 'These rules shall apply to *all* [author's stress] vessels upon the high seas and in all waters connected therewith navigable by seagoing vessels'.

At night, especially in coastal waters where shore lights add difficulty to the identification of other vessels, speed must be restricted to the point where the skipper is happy that he can stop, turn or take whatever action may be required regardless of the suddenness of events. If you are

Wake-jumping is stupid and dangerous in a big-ship channel.

not sure what speed to travel at, and you can slow down without diminishing your ability to manoeuvre then do so.

Many local authorities set specific speed limits within the confines of harbours and narrow channels and impose stiff penalties on those that break them – regardless of the size of the craft.

Rule 7

RISK OF COLLISION

(a) Every vessel shall use all available means appropriate to the prevailing circumstances and conditions to determine if risk of collision exists. If there is any doubt such risk shall be deemed to exist.

(b) Proper use shall be made of radar equipment if fitted and operational, including long-range scanning to obtain early warning of risk of collision and radar plotting or equivalent systematic observation of detected objects.

(c) Assumptions shall not be made on the basis of scanty information, especially scanty radar information.

(d) In determining if risk of collision exists the following considerations shall be among those taken into account:

(i) such risk shall be deemed to exist if the compass bearing of an approaching vessel does not appreciably change;

(ii) such risk may sometimes exist even when an appreciable bearing change is evident, particularly when

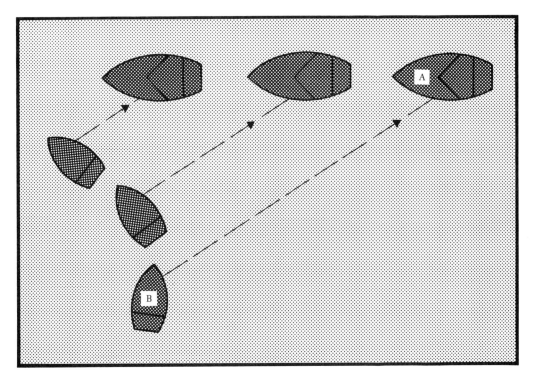

Even if the relative bearing between the two vessels alters quite considerably, if the magnetic bearing remains the same they will meet.

approaching a very large vessel or a tow or when approaching a vessel at close range.

Discussion on Rule 7

Rule 7 discusses the responsibility of every vessel to determine whether the risk of collision exists, and stipulates that if there is any doubt at all then the risk of collision should be deemed to exist.

Determining whether the risk of collision exists starts with the first sighting of another vessel. The first action should be to take a compass bearing of it. If this does not change then there is a risk of collision. Simultaneously when taking the first bearing, you should attempt to work out the approximate direction in which the other vessel is travelling and whether there may be any extenuating circumstances that may need to be considered. Are you in a narrow channel or in clear water? Is she likely to be considered a vessel that is limited in its ability to manoeuvre? Do you have rights over her in

terms of sail and power? Are you required 'not to impede' her passage? All of these questions must be asked and answered satisfactorily and as quickly as possible before deciding what action must be taken.

The rule also states that assumptions shall not be made on the basis of scanty information, especially scanty radar information. This again highlights the need to be properly conversant with your radar and what it can and does tell you. It is also an unfortunate fact that many collision situations are created by a tired or seasick crew member squinting through tired eyes and saying, 'It's OK, she's going the other way'.

At a distance, by day and without the benefit of seeing their lights, it is almost impossible to tell the direction of travel of some of the bigger cargo boats, especially the RO-ROs and car carriers. From a distance they look more like blocks of flats with no discernible bow, stern or bridge structure. Others, such as the really big bulk carriers, can appear to be two vessels

The yachts are sailing a bit too close to this ship for comfort.

until the long, low deck between the raised bow and the bridge on the after end comes into view at closer range.

Determining whether the risk of collision exists becomes easier with experience. The more you see other vessels at a distance the better you will become at identifying them and assessing the direction in which they are travelling. Even with this experience, however, it is important to keep a close eye on the situation until all danger or possibility of collision is well past.

The most complex situations can occur where commercial and pleasure craft meet at the entrances to harbours or estuaries. Rule 9 deals specifically with matters pertaining to narrow channels, but it is worth considering actions that can be taken to simplify the process of assessing whether the risk of collision may exist in crowded areas.

Before entering any new port or estuary you should have read the appropriate pilot book covering the area and also have had a good look at the chart. This will help you to determine the most likely courses that may be taken by both commercial and pleasure craft heading for or leaving their berths or marinas.

Many busy ports have small craft channels that are specifically designed to keep pleasure craft out of the way of the bigger commercial vessels. If these exist you should use them. But do beware that there may be places where the commercial craft have to cross the small craft channel to get to their berths.

Entering a new port or estuary area is a time for as many pairs of eyes being on lookout as possible. It is also useful to have someone at the chart table checking the finer details on the chart or in the pilot book. Most busy ports broadcast shipping

Channel marking buoys are not for mooring to.

movements that will be taking place within their confines on a regular basis on their appropriate VHF channels, and you should listen to this during your approach.

Having as much knowledge as possible of what goes on where in this kind of potentially congested area will contribute greatly to your ability to assess individual situations as they arise. But whatever the situation and however experienced the crew there is still no better way of telling whether the risk of collision exists than by taking a series of compass bearings of the other vessel. If the bearing does not change then risk of collision must be deemed to exist. If it does change it will tell you whether you will pass ahead or astern of the other vessel or whether there is a need for you to take any action to fulfil your responsibility to avoid a close-quarters situation.

Rule 8

ACTION TO AVOID COLLISION

(a)   Any action to avoid collision shall, if the circumstances of the case admit, be positive, made in ample time and with due regard to the observance of good seamanship.

(b)   Any alteration of course and/or speed to avoid collision shall, if the circumstances of the case admit, be large enough to be readily apparent to another vessel observing visually or by radar; a succession of small alterations of course and/or speed should be avoided.

(c)   If there is sufficient searoom, alteration of course alone may be the most effective action to avoid a close-quarters situation provided that it is made in good time, is substantial and does not result in another close-quarters situation.

(d)   Action taken to avoid collision with another vessel shall be such as to result in passing at a safe distance. The effectiveness of the action shall be carefully checked until the other vessel is finally past and clear.

(e)   If necessary to avoid collision or allow more time to assess the situation, a vessel shall slacken her speed or take all way off by stopping or reversing her means of propulsion.

(f)   (i)   A vessel which, by any of these Rules, is required not to impede the passage or safe passage of another vessel shall, when required by the circumstances of the case, take early action to allow sufficient searoom for the safe passage of the other vessel.

(ii)   A vessel required not to impede the passage or safe passage of another vessel is not relieved of this obligation if approaching the other vessel so as to involve risk of collision and shall, when taking action, have full regard to the action which may be required by the Rules of this part.

(iii)   A vessel the passage of which is not to be impeded remains fully obliged to comply with the Rules of this part when the two vessels are approaching one another so as to involve risk of collision.

Discussion on Rule 8

This is an entirely natural follow-on from Rule 7 and also acts as a preface to Rules 12 to 17 which stipulate what action must be taken and under what circumstances. Rule 8 really lays down the parameters of how action should be taken once the risk of collision or of a potential close-quarters situation has been deemed to exist.

The rule says that action should be taken 'in ample time'. In the sailing world there is a saying, 'The best time to reef is when you first think about it'. The same sentiment is true of taking action to avoid a collision. The sooner action is taken the less chance there will be of the development of a potentially dangerous close-quarters situation. By taking action as soon as you have ascertained that there is a risk of collision you give not only yourself but also the other vessel time to adjust to any other factors that may influence further movements.

Whatever you do it must be positive. This means that any course alteration should be such that the other vessel can clearly see what you have done. At night a course alteration should be such that the other vessel would see a change in the aspect of your lights. A course change of not less than 40 degrees should be sufficient.

If, for example, you were to alter course

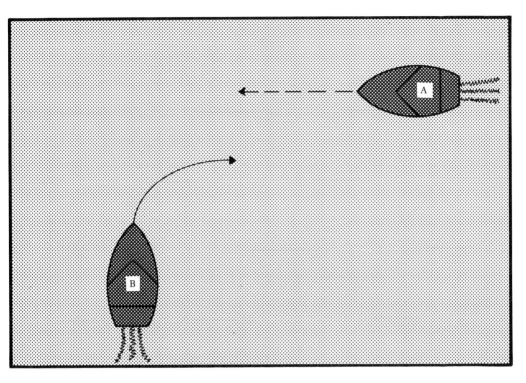

Course alterations must be positive and avoid crossing ahead of the other vessel.

to starboard to pass around the stern of a vessel sighted on your starboard bow this would result in him losing sight of your starboard light as you turn. He would then see your port side light and be in no doubt as to your actions. If you were to have made a small course alteration of say just 10 degrees you could still be showing him your starboard light and he would have no way of knowing that you had taken any action at all. The change in aspect of your lights would have been minimal even if you were under power and showing a steaming light.

This highlights one of the problems faced by the big ship watching a small boat without the benefit of high-quality radar. In anything apart from a very calm sea the heading of a small boat will not easily be apparent because the boat itself will be moved about by the action of the waves. Thus, only a major alteration of course will be sufficient to show the other vessel that positive action has been taken and it is not just the boat's head being thrown off course by a bigger wave or by the bad steering of an inattentive helmsman.

Rule 8 also says that any action taken should be such that it does not result in a further close-quarters situation developing. This and the need for the observance of good seamanship indicates that you should avoid crossing ahead of the vessel to which you are giving way. Crossing close ahead of another vessel in any situation is potentially highly dangerous. This is because the other vessel cannot possibly know for certain whether you are actually going to continue across his bows. He may feel obliged to take some kind of avoiding action which could ultimately lead to a collision.

Whatever action is taken or contemplated, it should be based upon all of the factors that are evident. There is no point in taking action to avoid someone if the action you have taken immediately creates a potentially dangerous situation either with yet another vessel or to your own through the proximity of other dangers such as rocks or shallows.

Rule 8 also suggests that slowing down or even stopping cannot only help avoid the risk of collision but can also give more time to assess the situation. Far too few people ever actually think of doing this. In a power boat it is easy enough, although it may result in a less comfortable ride for a brief period of time. In a sailing vessel, depending on the point of sail and the weather, it should not pose a problem to ease the sheets or even to heave-to.

A minute or so spent travelling at slower speed will easily be sufficient to take stock of the situation, and the speed change should also bring about a change in the aspect or bearing of the other vessel. It must, however, be borne in mind that a small alteration of speed will not readily be apparent to the other vessel, especially if it is the difference between sailing at 5 knots and pinching at 2 knots.

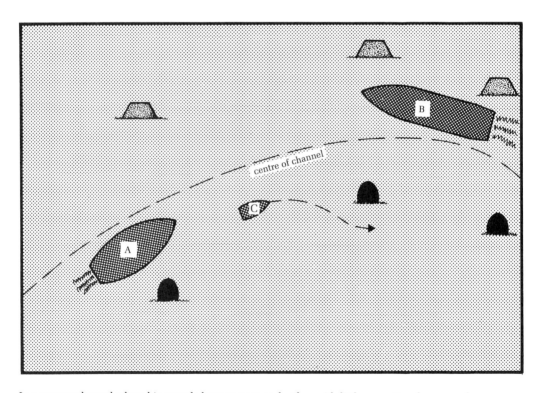

In a narrow channel where big vessels have to pass each other with little room it makes sense for small craft like C here to move out of the channel if there is sufficient water to give space for A as she passes B.

Trip boats on the Thames should keep to the starboard side of the channel but in any big river beware because they do suddenly dive across to their piers and can travel at some speed.

In a narrow channel or otherwise confined waters the safest and often the easiest action to take, if the other vessel is much bigger than you, is to move just outside the main channel where you will have enough water but he probably would not. This situation would be helped by having a crew member at the chart table who can give instant advice as to any potential hazards that may be encountered should this action need to be taken. In many instances this is where you should be anyway, presuming there is sufficient water for you.

The last part (f) of Rule 8 has recently been added to clarify the situation where vessels meeting may be required to 'keep out of the way of' and/or 'not impede' the other. However, the situation may arise where the vessel whose passage is not to be impeded may, within the context of the rules, be the vessel that should give way if a close-quarters situation should develop. If such a situation should develop it could well be because the smaller vessel did not make way for the other as she should have done. This is most likely to occur either in a traffic separation scheme or in a narrow channel where the smaller vessel is in the act of crossing the channel or the separation lane. For the small-boat skipper this highlights the importance of careful

The yacht is bearing away to cross the channel behind the ferry and the car transporter, which is travelling in the same direction as the ferry believe it or not.

planning to choose the right moment to cross in safety well clear of any other vessels. This leads us directly into the requirements of Rule 9 which deals specifically with the conduct of vessels in narrow channels.

Narrow Channels

The small-craft skipper will face more problems related to the rules of the road in narrow channels used by both commercial and pleasure craft than he will ever meet off the coast or out at sea. At sea the movements of most vessels will be reasonably predictable as most will follow a set course and travel at a constant speed. In the channels that lead to and from major ports or around popular parts of the coast where the greatest concentration of shipping is to be found, nothing can be totally predictable. To look at some of the problems and potential dangers that are to

be encountered in such areas I spent some time on patrol in the waters adjacent to Southampton on board the harbour master's patrol launch *Millbrook*.

Millbrook is a 13m (42ft) Weymouth with a maximum speed of about 18 knots. She covers a patch that includes the Rivers Itchen and Test, Southampton Water itself and the Central Solent between Cowes and Calshot. With a crew of two, a patrol officer and a coxswain, she is on the water twenty-four hours a day and carries out a variety of tasks from checking navigational aids such as lights and buoys to escorting the bigger ships into and out of the area.

During the patrol it became apparent that just a small percentage of pleasure-craft skippers caused most of the problems while the rest enjoyed themselves safely and sensibly. This small percentage of skippers of both sailing and power boats paid scant regard to the requirements of either the rules of the road themselves or

The harbour master's launch keeps the channel clear for a container ship.

The *Millbrook* passing a yacht lowering sail in the main channel.

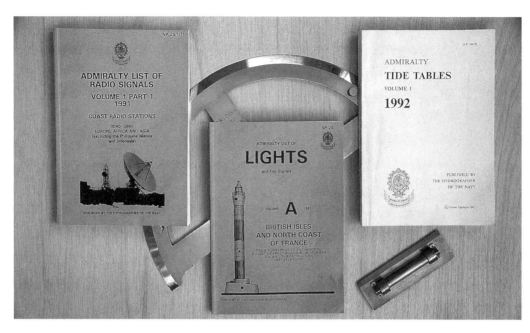

Apart from charts there are many publications that can help the mariner to ensure he stays in safe waters and has advance knowledge of any special navigational needs.

the special regulations governing speeds and use of the main channels by small craft within this area. What was surprising was that many of the pleasure craft that were seen and admonished for breaking the rules were being handled by neither beginners nor hooligans.

This did not, however, surprise the crew on the *Millbrook*. Both the patrol officer and the coxswain had many stories of seemingly incredible stupidity and pigheadedness by people that most would have expected to know better. One incident involved a 20m (60ft) ketch anchored in the middle of the Thorne Channel while the owner and his guests had tea. A polite request to up-anchor and move to make way for a large commercial vessel was met with the curt reply that the boat would be moved after the company on board had finished their tea. Further more strongly worded requests were also refused. In the end the patrol boat put a grappling iron on board and towed the vessel, complete with dragging anchor, out of the channel. The patrol officer in the launch took this action as a last resort to safeguard the boat and its crew and ensure safe passage for the oncoming cargo vessel.

Another incident concerned a senior flag officer of an old established yacht club who would not move his 15m (50ft) ketch out of the main channel to give way to a supertanker saying that power should give way to sail. On that occasion the patrol boat stopped across the bows of the ketch and forced him to move out of the channel.

These are true and well-documented stories that really illustrate a pathetic and outdated attitude of stupidity by people that appear to have no understanding of the possible repercussions of their actions.

Yacht clubs themselves also came in for some criticism. Start lines for races were regularly laid across main channels without any attempt to check on ship movements in advance. Committee boats marking one end of a start or finish line were often found anchored within the main channels. As the patrol officer pointed out a telephone or radio call to the Southampton Vessel Traffic Services (VTS) to check on traffic movements would avoid embarrassment for the club, and more importantly potential danger for those competing in the race.

Even before starting the patrol from the Dockhead at the confluence of the Rivers Test and Itchen we found our first offender. A 10m (30ft) power boat emerged from one of the marinas on the Itchen and took off towards Southampton Water, right past the patrol launch and at a speed of about 25 knots. Stopped by the *Millbrook* sounding its two-tone horn, the power boat's skipper said that he had been under the impression that the speed limit only came into force above the Itchen Bridge. The patrol officer on the *Millbrook* was scathing. 'He should know where the speed restriction area starts because he keeps his boat here' he said. 'Also, driving at that speed, and kicking up the kind of wash that he does, close to a lot of small boat moorings, is dangerous as well as just plain thoughtless.'

He did say that while the majority of power boat drivers stuck to the rules there were still too many that did not consider the problems that their speed and wash could cause in enclosed or restricted waters. He felt that this type of helmsman appeared to have little or no concern for the safety and well-being of others – especially when passing too close, too fast and with little or no regard for the comfort or safety of people in small craft. 'They

Some power boat drivers are thoughtless when passing close to small yachts.

may not be breaking the rules of the road as such,' said the patrol officer, 'but they are certainly not complying with the spirit of the rules which requires everyone to conduct their vessels in a seamanlike manner.'

Millbrook's next task was to patrol the channel in front of a 250,000 tonne supertanker from its berth at the Esso Terminal, around Calshot and the Thorne Channel and then to see it clear of Cowes. Four large tugs were making their lines fast to the tanker as we arrived off its berth.

As the last of the shorelines were cast off a big, new-looking ketch sailed slowly across the channel from the mouth of the Hamble directly towards the tugs. Her

skipper seemed surprised when *Mill-brook*, with two-tone horn going, moved alongside and requested them to turn back and clear out of the main channel. Despite the obvious activity going on around the supertanker they said they had not realized that it was about to leave its berth. Their boathandling was as unskilful as their perception and observation, and in a boat worth at least £145,000 one would have expected it to be better. Many small-boat skippers do not realize the extent of the turbulence that can exist in the vicinity of a big ship when it is leaving or arriving at a berth. If there is any wind blowing there will often be up to three or four tugs pushing or pulling and the wash from

Navigational hazards must be taken into account when avoiding close-quarter situations.

(a) He had to get his spinnaker down in a hurry to get out of the channel . . .

their propellers can be incredibly strong and reach some way out into the channel.

As the tanker pulled away from the berth, helped by its attendant tugs, *Millbrook* took up a position in the middle of the channel about three cables ahead of her. This was about the minimum distance ahead where she could be seen from the tanker's bridge. This in itself illustrated just how restricted the view can be from some of these big ships, especially when they are high out of the water having just discharged their cargo.

During the next thirty minutes we had to tell some fifteen boats, large and small, power and sail, to clear the channel – including, once again, the big ketch that we had met earlier. Her crew had trouble getting themselves and the sails organized to go about, and in the end they were summarily told to start their engine and move out of the channel.

Returning from this patrol we found a windsurfer in the water beside his board

(b) . . . and this is the reason . . .

(c) . . . he had to be chased out of the channel.

on the edge of the channel just off Calshot spit. He did not want to accept a lift so we stood by and saw him safely across the channel. Both the patrol officer and the coxswain felt that windsurfers were a danger to both themselves and others when they sailed close to or across the main channels. The problem is that when they do come off their boards and their sails lie flat in the water they are difficult to see even if their sails are brightly coloured.

In all of these incidents, none of the small boats concerned should have been within the channels at all. Apart from specific local requisitions which ban small vessels from certain areas of the deep-water channels when big ships are in the approaches or in the channels themselves, they were all contravening section (b) of Rule 9. This requires vessels of less than 20m (22ft) or sailing vessels not to impede the passage of a vessel which can safely navigate only within a narrow channel or fairway. Many obviously did not realize that most of the big ships travelled at between 7 knots and 15 knots or more depending on tides and their individual characteristics and requirements for man-oeuvrability. Many people that sail really do not like to put their engines on between leaving one berth and arriving at another. This is fine, but when close to big ship channels when strong tides are running it is good seamanship to use the engine if that is what is needed to keep clear of the channel and avoid difficulties for larger vessels.

Another aspect of the use of the channels in this area was the endless number of

This picture was taken from outside the channel. The other yacht should not have been there.

small craft – both power and sail – travelling up and down in the middle of the deep-water channel in Southampton Water itself. This happened despite there being plenty of water on either side of the channel at any state of the tide. Most of these boats were breaking section (a) of Rule 9 requiring all vessels to keep as far over to the starboard side of a narrow channel as is safe and practicable. They were also contravening Section (b) of the same rule. It was almost as though they were setting out to make things as difficult as possible for themselves considering the numbers of ferries travelling to and fro. These ferries included catamarans, hydrofoils and hovercraft some of which were travelling at speeds of up to 45 knots. By staying outside the main channel the small craft would have had considerably less to worry about in terms of being run down, although even the ferries and hovercraft keep out of the main channel when either a very large vessel or a gas tanker is in the fairway.

Gas tankers always get special treatment because of the hazardous cargo they carry and it is worth being able to recognize them. They are not specifically very large but are often painted orange or yellow and some have bulbous tank tops on their main deck. When they are in the vicinity everything else is required to keep out of the channel they are using.

Gas tankers get priority.

During the remainder of the patrol, which included another two passages to clear the channel in front of large commercial vessels, we saw further evidence of both the good and the bad in seamanship and boat handling. The stream of small craft continued to stick to the centre of the main channels and several times we heard big ships and ferries sounding five short blasts. This officially means that one vessel is in doubt as to whether the other is taking sufficient action to avoid collision, but when boiled down to basics in this situation it usually means 'get out of my way'.

Small-boat skippers that act as if the main channels and their associated buoyage systems exist purely for the benefit of the big ships and have little or no relevance to them endanger not only themselves but every other craft in the area. The way a small-boat skipper conducts his boat in and around narrow channels highlights his skills or his thoughtlessness. Narrow channels should be treated with respect by all.

Although the events described happened in one very crowded area, it could have been anywhere. What it clearly illustrated was that those who stuck by the rules in letter and in spirit had fun while those who did not had problems.

Rule 9

NARROW CHANNELS

(a) A vessel proceeding along the course of a narrow channel or fairway shall keep as near to the outer limit of the channel or fairway which lies on her starboard side as is safe and practicable.

(b) A vessel of less than 20 metres in length or a sailing vessel shall not impede the passage of a vessel which can safely navigate only within a narrow channel or fairway.

(c) A vessel engaged in fishing shall not impede the passage of any other vessel navigating within a narrow channel or fairway.

(d) A vessel shall not cross a narrow channel or fairway if such crossing impedes the passage of a vessel which can safely navigate only within such channel or fairway. The latter vessel may use the sound signal prescribed in Rule 34(d) if in doubt as to the intention of the crossing vessel.

(e) (i) In a narrow channel or fairway when overtaking can take place only if the vessel to be overtaken has to take action to permit safe passing, the vessel intending to overtake shall indicate her intention by sounding the appropriate signal prescribed in Rule 34(c)(i). The vessel to be overtaken shall, if in agreement, sound the appropriate signal prescribed in Rule 34(c)(ii) and take steps to permit safe passing. If in doubt she may sound the signals prescribed in Rule 34(d).

(ii) This Rule does not relieve the overtaking vessel of her obligation under Rule 13.

(f) A vessel nearing a bend or an area of a narrow channel or fairway where other vessels may be obscured by an intervening obstruction shall navigate with particular alertness and caution and shall sound the appropriate signal prescribed in Rule 34(e).

(g) Any vessel shall, if the circumstances of the case admit, avoid anchoring in a narrow channel.

Discussion on Rule 9

A narrow channel to a supertanker may be a whole sailing ground to a small boat. It is a relative term and the rule itself does not attempt to define it further. However, in the context of the rule it may be assumed that a narrow channel is one that is marked by port and starboard hand buoys or other

No channel marks in sight but the yachts and the hydrofoil pass safely port to port by staying on the starboard side of the approach channel.

Big ships passing in a narrow channel often have little room for error.

markers, or is closely bounded by river or canal banks that obviously limit the direction of travel.

In essence, the rule says that everyone should keep as well over to the starboard side of the channel as is practicable for their vessel and that smaller boats should keep clear of big ones.

The second section of the rule quite clearly provides priority for larger vessels, especially those that may be restricted by their draught or in their ability to man-oeuvre such that they have to keep to the deepest parts of the channel. It specifically states that sailing vessels of any size and all vessels of less than 20m (66ft) *shall not* impede the passage of these larger vessels. This is another of those occasions where power does not give way to sail.

The small-boat skipper must therefore keep a good lookout for larger vessels, and wherever possible must keep his boat as nearly as may be safe and practicable on

the extreme edge of the main channel – or if possible, outside it. This is also a time when it is critically important to keep a good lookout astern as well as ahead, especially where the channel twists and turns between banks that limit visibility. Remember that the intervening banks or buildings on the corners of the channel may cut down the sound of approaching vessels who may not always give sound signals as they approach each turn in the channel.

The small-boat skipper must also be aware of the dangers of fast flowing currents and tidal streams within the confines of narrow channels. Remember that in general terms the fastest streams and deepest water will be found on the outside sections of the bends – usually this will be the route of the main buoyed channels – with the slower streams and shallows on the inside sections of the bends. Once again, complying with the

Keep the channel markers between yourself and the big ships wherever possible.

Don't look now but you are being followed – do they know?

rules will be made easier if you have had a good look at the chart and the pilotage notes for the area in your almanac or pilot book. Knowing what to expect means being prepared. This means that decisions to change course or move outside or across a buoyed channel can be made with confidence at the right time, in the right place and with safety.

It is very important to know and understand the sound signals that may be heard whether they are those in Rule 9 or whether they are special signals for that area that have been made under Rule 1(b) – these will usually be found in the pilot book for the area.

Most power boats have built-in horns that can be operated from the helm position, but few sailing boats have this facility so it makes sense for them to have their portable fog-horns ready to hand in the cockpit when navigating in narrow channels. It may not be necessary to give sound signals to the big ships, but other small boats may need to be reminded of your presence or advised of your intentions.

What is not generally understood by the majority of small-boat skippers is that big ships in narrow channels are usually steering to very specific and carefully planned courses from which they can not safely deviate. Their need to allow for tidal flow and to keep to a specific track when negotiating sharp turns is critical. Once committed to a sharp turn even at a relatively slow speed it can be extremely difficult for them to make further course changes without actually leaving the main channel. In this situation most big ships will travel somewhat faster than their minimum safe speed below which they cannot be steered with any degree of control. The minimum safe speed for large passenger and cargo vessels can be anything between 7 knots and 12 knots which is faster than the average sailing boat or displacement motor cruiser. To expect a large vessel to deviate in any way from its course in these circumstances is foolhardy in the extreme. But it is

Ferry skippers get used to yachts in the main channel, but other big ships may be less tolerant.

an unfortunate fact that there are still some people that believe that power should give way to sail in any situation. Tragically their numbers tend to decrease as a direct result of their beliefs.

The possible consequences of a supertanker or cruise liner having to go off course and subsequently run aground on the Bramble Bank in the middle of the Solent are not pleasant to contemplate. Most big ships only have a single layer of bottom plates and these form the base of their fuel tanks. If these were to be fractured the ecological disaster would be such that the 50,000 pleasure boats that currently enjoy the Solent area would suddenly have nowhere to go that was not oil drenched and ruined.

So, the final message here is keep your eyes open, stay out of the main channel if you safely can, and whatever you do, keep out of the way of the big ships.

Traffic Separation Schemes

Before discussing Rule 10 and its specific requirements it is worth taking a closer look at what Traffic Separation Schemes actually are, who should use them and how, and how they and the vessels using them are monitored.

Traffic Separation Schemes (TSS) were conceived to facilitate the safe passage of all vessels in restricted areas of exceptionally high traffic density. In British and Continental waters many such schemes exist. They include those in the Straits of Dover, in mid-Channel to the north-west of the Channel Islands, off the Brittany coast at Ushant and around Land's End and the Scilly Isles. Because of the numbers, size and speed of the commercial vessels that use these schemes it is important that the small-boat skipper fully understands how to traverse or use them safely.

Traffic Separation Schemes are to be found in many places around the world and are clearly shown on nautical charts. They are designed to keep traffic which is proceeding in opposite or nearly opposite directions in separate lanes by the use of separation zones or lines like the central reservation of a land-based motorway or dual carriageway. Many of the schemes also incorporate Inshore Traffic Zones that are specifically designated areas essentially for the use of small craft travelling in any direction, but which larger vessels may also use under specific circumstances.

The lanes themselves, the adjacent Inshore Traffic Zones and the separation zones or separation lines are all clearly defined on the charts of the area. Only vessels actually crossing the area covered by the separation scheme or vessels that are fishing are permitted into the separation zones or across the separation lines.

Britain led the world in creating the concept of Traffic Separation Schemes. The concept of creating one-way traffic lanes came about in an effort to cut down the numbers of collisions that were occurring in the Dover Strait. By the early 1960s this had become extremely congested as a result of the increase in the volume, size and speed of traffic to and from the ports of northern Europe. The idea, which resulted in the creation of the first ever TSS, was implemented in the Dover Strait on a voluntary basis in 1967. Its success was highlighted by a marked reduction in the number of collisions and in 1972, following approval by the IMO,

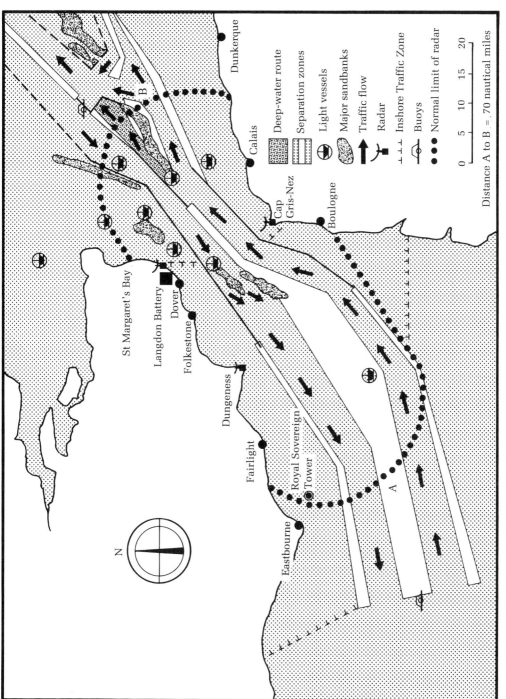

The Traffic Separation Scheme in the Dover Strait.

Deep-water route
Separation zones
Light vessels
Major sandbanks
Traffic flow
Radar
Inshore Traffic Zone
Buoys
Normal limit of radar

Distance A to B = .70 nautical miles

0   5   10   15   20

Dunkerque
Calais
Cap Gris-Nez
Boulogne
St Margaret's Bay
Langdon Battery
Dover
Folkestone
Dungeness
Fairlight
Royal Sovereign Tower
Eastbourne

N

A
B

the scheme in the Dover Strait became compulsory for British ships. In 1977 the introduction of the revised collision regulations made it mandatory for ships of all nations.

A further safety measure for vessels traversing the Dover Strait was added in 1979 when the MAREP reporting system was introduced. This involved all vessels carrying certain grades of potentially dangerous cargoes like oil, chemicals or gas, or those restricted in their ability to manoeuvre or not under command being invited to report to Dover Coastguard when they entered the area of the TSS. This enables the coastguard to keep track of their movements and ensures that their masters are notified of any potential problems in their way. Other vessels in the TSS are notified of the presence of these vessels and are requested to give them clear passage.

In any given twenty-four-hour period in the Dover Strait, an average of 300 vessels travel up or down through the scheme in the lanes themselves. In the same period there can also be up to 200 cross-Channel ferry movements across the lanes. This includes the high-speed hovercraft travelling at anything up to 65 knots, the new fast catamarans and the more traditional car and passenger ferries, but it does not include small craft or fishing boats.

What the small-boat skipper has to

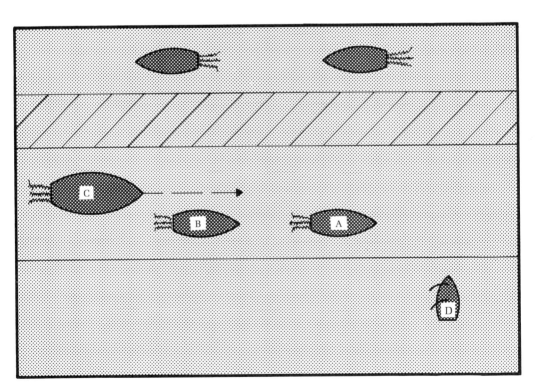

A sailing yacht or slow-speed motor cruiser D may think of crossing behind A and in front of B but may get caught by C which is travelling faster than the others. It pays to observe for a few minutes before crossing a busy traffic lane.

realize is that whilst the vessels in any given traffic lane will, or should be, all travelling in the same direction their speeds may vary enormously. A line of vessels may initially appear to be travelling at similar speeds but a couple of minutes' observation may well show that some are overtaking others rapidly. While the majority of vessels will probably be travelling at between 10 and 20 knots, a fair number will be travelling considerably faster than this and some will be rather slower. This means that lane crossing must be done with care and with as many pairs of eyes on lookout as possible. In many instances the local coastguard can help with information on shipping movements. Ships often travel in groups because they are aiming to catch a

tide or have just left on one. Those schemes that are monitored by a coastguard service radar will be able to advise over VHF where there are heavy traffic flows and where there are gaps.

The TSS in the Dover Strait is probably the most sophisticated in the world. It is certainly the busiest. Dover Coastguard monitor every movement within an area about 65km (40 miles) each side of Folkestone and across the full width of the Channel from the Langdon Battery Operations Centre on the cliffs above Dover. On the French side similar coverage is carried out from Cap Gris-Nez. Dover Coastguard also provide a twenty-four-hour radio safety service for all shipping in the Dover Strait. This is called the Channel Navigation Information

Keeping watch over the Dover Strait Traffic Separation Scheme at the Langdon Battery Radar Room.

Coastguard Station Officer Eric Musson has a good view of Dover Harbour from the Langdon Battery.

Service and broadcasts are made on VHF Channel 11 every hour (or thirty minutes in poor visibility) to give warnings of navigational difficulties such as vessels that may be restricted in their ability to manoeuvre, survey or salvage ships working in the area, misplaced or defective navigational aids and exceptional tidal or weather conditions. This kind of service will not be available at all schemes but where it is it will be noted in the pilot book for the area.

Radar operators watch the movements of every vessel in the area of the TSS. They keep careful track of all the vessels using the MAREP voluntary Ship Movement Reporting Scheme. They also watch closely for any contraventions of the collision regulations by any vessel using the TSS and also those crossing the scheme or using the Inshore Traffic Zone. Anyone that looks as though they may be straying off course, taking a route across the scheme that is not at right angles to the flow of traffic, or otherwise not complying with the regulations is carefully monitored and their movements recorded. Offenders are called up by radio and asked to confirm their identity, position and course and speed. Sometimes they have wandered through error, but those that blatantly contravene the regulations are visually identified by aircraft at the direction of the Coastguard.

Details of contraventions of the international collision regulations are forwarded to the Marine Directorate of the Department of Transport along with evidence of the contravention in the form of video recordings of the radar coverage plus a full report of any communications between vessels or with the coastguard. This is all carefully analysed by the experts at the department and a decision taken as to whether action should be taken against the offending vessel.

The Marine Directorate of the Department of Transport takes proceedings against offending British registered vessels, but details of contraventions of the regulations by foreign registered vessels are forwarded to their own flag state for action to be taken there. This also relates to small pleasure craft and fishing vessels.

The rules governing the use of Traffic Separation Schemes are not immensely complex but the results or penalties for breaking them can be fatal in the worst circumstance or at the least expensive should action be brought for an offence.

Rule 10

TRAFFIC SEPARATION SCHEMES

(a) This rule applies to traffic separation schemes adopted by the Organization and does not relieve any vessel of her obligation under any other rule.

(b) A vessel using a traffic separation scheme shall:

(i) proceed in the appropriate traffic lane in the general direction of traffic flow for that lane;

(ii) so far as practicable keep clear of a traffic separation line or separation zone;

(iii) normally join or leave a traffic lane at the termination of the lane, but when joining or leaving from either side shall do so at as small an angle to the general direction of traffic flow as practicable.

(c) A vessel shall, so far as practicable, avoid crossing traffic lanes but if obliged to do so shall cross on a heading as nearly as practicable at right angles to the general direction of traffic flow.

(d) (i) A vessel shall not use an inshore traffic zone when she can safely use the appropriate traffic lane within the adjacent traffic separation scheme. However, vessels of less than 20 metres in length, sailing vessels and vessels engaged in fishing may use the inshore traffic zone.

(ii) Notwithstanding subparagraph (d)(i), a vessel may use an inshore traffic zone when *en route* to or from a port, offshore installation or structure, pilot station or any other place situated within the inshore traffic zone, or to avoid immediate danger.

(e) A vessel other than a crossing vessel or a vessel joining or leaving a lane shall not normally enter a separation zone or cross a separation line except:

(i) in cases of emergency to avoid immediate danger;

(ii) to engage in fishing within a separation zone.

(f) A vessel navigating in areas near the terminations of traffic separation schemes shall do so with particular caution.

(g) A vessel shall so far as practicable avoid anchoring in a traffic separation scheme or in areas near its terminations.

(h) A vessel not using a traffic separation scheme shall avoid it by as wide a margin as is practicable.

(i)   A vessel engaged in fishing shall not impede the passage of any vessel following a traffic lane.

(j)   A vessel of less than 20 metres in length or a sailing vessel shall not impede the safe passage of a power-driven vessel following a traffic lane.

(k)   A vessel restricted in her ability to manoeuvre when engaged in an operation for the maintenance of safety of navigation in a traffic separation scheme is exempted from complying with this Rule to the extent necessary to carry out the operation.

(l)   A vessel restricted in her ability to manoeuvre when engaged in an operation for the laying, servicing or picking up of a submarine cable, within a traffic separation scheme, is exempted from complying with this Rule to the extent necessary to carry out the operation.

Discussion on Rule 10

Essentially the rule requires vessels using the traffic lanes to keep to them and to travel in the general direction of the traffic flow without getting close to the subdividing lines or separation zones. It also requires vessels that join the scheme from anywhere but the ends of the lanes to do so at as small an angle as possible so as to meld easily into the general traffic flow. This clearly shows any other vessel that may be watching visually or by radar that the vessel entering the lane intends to travel with the general flow of traffic and

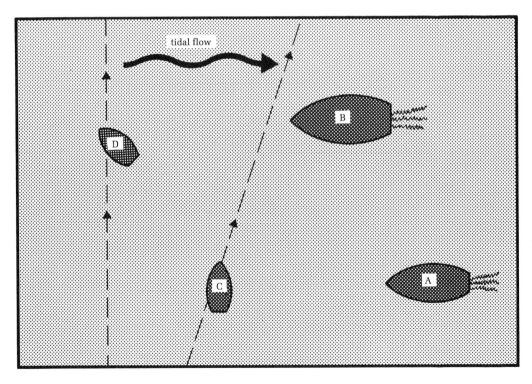

tidal flow

Crossing the TSS the proper way. A can see that yacht C is crossing the lane, whereas B may think that D is proceeding up the lane but keeping an erratic course.

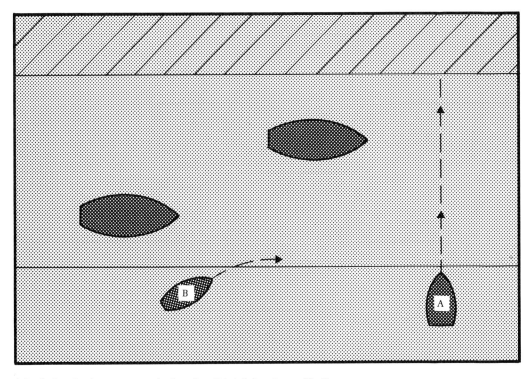

A is obviously about to cross the lane but B is joining the traffic flow.

is not intending to cross the lane.

A vessel that does intend to cross the lane or the scheme as a whole must do so on a heading that is as nearly as possible at right angles to the direction of flow of the traffic. This keeps the time a crossing vessel is in the lane to a minimum irrespective of the tidal stream, and clearly shows other vessels its direction of travel by night or by day. For some time there was confusion as to whether the vessel's heading or its actual ground track had to be at right angles to the traffic flow. The confusion is now over as it is clearly defined in section (c) of Rule 10 that it is the heading that must be at right angles to the flow. In other words, the vessel will present itself beam on to any vessels using the traffic lane. As all are equally affected by any tide that may be flowing this also helps to equalize comparative movements and speeds.

Given the speed and density of traffic that is liable to be found in most Traffic Separation Schemes the best advice to the small-boat skipper is to stay away from them where possible. Few small pleasure craft and very few sailing vessels are capable of sustaining the speeds at which the majority of commercial vessels travel. This is especially true if the weather is anything but favourable and the sea state heavier than moderate. Where a sailing vessel is crossing the scheme she should do so as quickly as possible. A sailing vessel with an auxiliary engine should make use of it if the winds are light or if she has a difficulty in maintaining a heading that is close to right angles to the traffic flow.

Subsection (j) of Rule 10 clearly points out that a sailing vessel does not have right of way over a power-driven vessel using a TSS. She is in fact specifically required not to impede the safe passage of a power-driven vessel that is using the lanes. What must be borne in mind is that in a traffic lane there may be a queue of vessels travelling within a mile or less of each other. Should any of them have to make a sudden course alteration this may require any or all of the others to do likewise. This could be exceedingly dangerous especially if there is little separation between the lanes.

As far as the Inshore Traffic Zones are concerned, the small-boat skipper still needs to keep a careful lookout for larger vessels, especially in the vicinity of coastal ports. He or she must also remember that traffic of all kinds may be travelling in any direction in these areas as there is no specific direction of flow.

As a final thought, it must be remembered that use of the scheme in accordance with Rule 10 does not in any way alter the overriding requirements for vessels to comply with the other rules of the regulations. The content of subsection (j) does not in fact alter the requirements for all vessels to follow the rest of the rules should a close-quarters situation arise and this is highlighted in Rule 8(f)(iii).

Section II – Conduct of Vessels in Sight of One Another

This is arguably the most important section of the rules as far as the small-boat skipper is concerned, because the majority of his or her decisions and actions will be taken following the visual sighting of another vessel. In our crowded coastal waters where vessels of all types will be encountered regularly, action to avoid close-quarters situations must be taken quickly and positively. The small-boat skipper must be able to identify the other vessels in the vicinity quickly, judge whether he or she needs to take avoiding action and assess the most appropriate action to take that will keep him or her clear of any and all other vessels in the area.

At sea, few small-boat skippers will ever be in a position where they may have to decide whether or not to make a course alteration for a vessel that is out of sight over the horizon even if they are equipped with radar. Assuming a height of eye of 2–5m (6.5–16.5ft) which probably covers the majority of sailing boats and medium-sized flybridge power boats, this will give a visible horizon distance of 2.5–5 miles (4–8km) in good visibility. This means that the small-boat skipper may not have much time to decide upon what action to take once another vessel has been sighted. The worst situation is a head-on or nearly head-on meeting with a large vessel which may be travelling at anything up to 30 knots. This would give a skipper with a 4 mile (6.5km) horizon rather less than seven minutes, assuming he is himself travelling at 6 knots, before he found himself in the same piece of water as up to 250,000 tonnes of opposing force. Seven minutes may seem a long time to some, but it is frightening how quickly it runs out when bearings have to be taken and actions decided upon.

It is this kind of situation that highlights

the need for the small-boat skipper to really master this section of the rules. He or she must have no doubt as to the appropriate action to be considered or taken wherever there is the possibility of a close-quarters situation arising.

Rule 11

APPLICATION
Rules in this section apply to vessels in sight of one another.

Discussion on Rule 11

This rule emphasizes the fact that the rules in Section II relate to situations where vessels are visible to each other by the naked eye. They do not relate to situations where vessels are seen on radar alone.

Is this a power-driven vessel?

Rule 12

SAILING VESSELS
(a)   When two sailing vessels are approaching one another, so as to involve risk of collision, one of them shall keep out of the away of the other as follows:
    (i)   when each has the wind on a different side, the vessel which has the wind on the port side shall keep out of the way of the other;
    (ii)   when both have the wind on the same side, the vessel which is to windward shall keep out of the way of the vessel which is to leeward;
    (iii)   if a vessel with the wind on the port side sees a vessel to windward and cannot determine with certainty whether the other vessel has the wind on the port or on the starboard side, she shall keep out of the way of the other.
(b)   For the purpose of this Rule the windward side shall be deemed to be the side opposite to that on which the mainsail is carried or, in the case of a square-rigged vessel, the side opposite to that on which the largest fore-and-aft sail is carried.

Discussion on Rule 12

Here it must be remembered that a sailing vessel using her engine is deemed to be a power-driven vessel whether she also has sails up or not. If she has sails set she should be showing the appropriate signal (black cone with point facing downwards) as required in Rule 25(e), and is therefore governed by the other rules in the steering and sailing section relating to power-driven vessels.

Sections (a)(i) and (a)(ii) of this rule are perfectly straightforward. Section (a)(iii) is a recent addition that was made to

From here you can see that this yacht is on the port tack but it would not be easy from further ahead and further away.

resolve the problem of identifying on which tack a windward vessel may be. This is especially difficult at night when it is impossible to see which side the mainsail is on. Even by day at a distance when the windward vessel has a spinnaker up it can be difficult to make a positive judgement until the spinnaker pole itself or the mainsail can be seen. By that stage it may be too late to take sufficient action to avoid a collision. Section (a)(iii) of Rule 12 now places the onus of responsibility to take action squarely on the close-hauled vessel who must assume that the vessel running is on the starboard tack and therefore has right of way.

Although Rule 12 is directed primarily at sailing vessels it is important that power boat skippers understand what it may mean to them. This is especially important in areas where numbers of sailing vessels heading in different directions may be

Faced with this lot it would be a brave or foolish man that claimed his right of way on starboard if he was not part of the same race.

encountered. In the Solent, the Clyde, around the south-west of Britain and in other highly populated sailing areas it is not uncommon to find large racing fleets. Where possible it is safest and indeed courteous to give these a wide berth. Sailing vessels that are racing will normally be flying a racing pennant of some type in place of the national ensign. Usually their courses are marked out by conspicuous yellow buoys. Offshore start and finish lines can be identified by the presence of an official vessel flying various flags and pennants at one end of the line and a buoy of some type at the other. However, boats that are racing are still bound in every way by the contents of these rules but in the heat of competition they may well leave their course changes very late indeed and might not always make the most obvious moves.

All power boat skippers should have sufficient knowledge of the basics of sailing to understand what course changes may be made by sailing boats. This will help in every situation as well as when taking the appropriate avoiding action required as a power-driven vessel giving way to a sailing vessel under the requirements of Rule 18. For the power boat skipper without a knowledge of sailing a brief outline of some of the relevant terms and factors related to the main points of sail are given below.

A sailing boat is said to be close-hauled or beating when she is heading as close as possible into the wind. How close will vary with the boat and the existing weather conditions, but the average sailing boat will head to within about 40 degrees of the direction from which the wind is coming. A boat that is close-hauled or beating will have both the mainsail and the foresail or jib pulled in

as close to the centreline of the boat as possible. The boat will also be heeled over which can create a blind arc for the helmsman on his lee side (the side on which the sails are set) where his view may be blanketed by the foresail. There should be someone sitting down to leeward in the cockpit to keep a lookout over this blind arc, but it is as well to assume that you have not been seen until you have positively identified someone looking at you. On this point of sail, however, in reasonable sea conditions most sailing boats are able to change course with the minimum of problems.

A sailing boat is said to be running free or running before the wind when she is sailing with the wind coming from directly astern of her. In this situation she may have her mainsail set out to one side with her foresail out on the other. She may have a spinnaker set. This latter is a large, usually brightly coloured sail that is roughly triangular and set from the top of the mast directly in front of the boat. On this point of sail, and especially with a spinnaker set, it can be difficult and indeed dangerous for the boat to have to make a sudden change of course.

In between close-hauled and running free when the wind is anywhere between 40 degrees on the bow and say 10 degrees off being directly astern, the boat is said to be reaching. This is when a sailing boat will achieve its maximum speed. Both main and foresail will be on the same side of the boat, and depending on whether it is a broad reach or a close reach they will be relatively further out from the centreline. The boat may also carry a reacher or cruising chute. This resembles a spinnaker but is carried on one side of the boat only, and may limit the ability of the boat to make sudden changes of course.

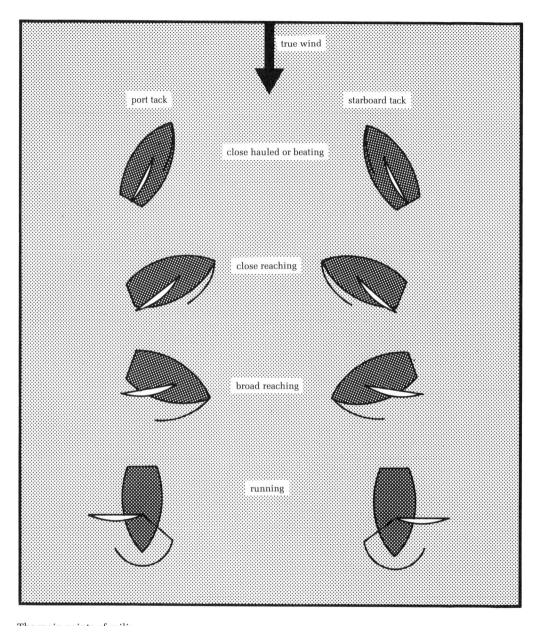

The main points of sailing.

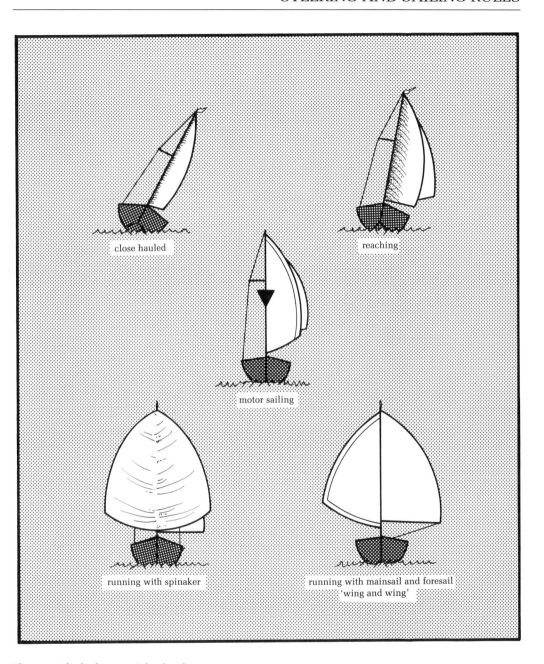

The way it looks from straight ahead.

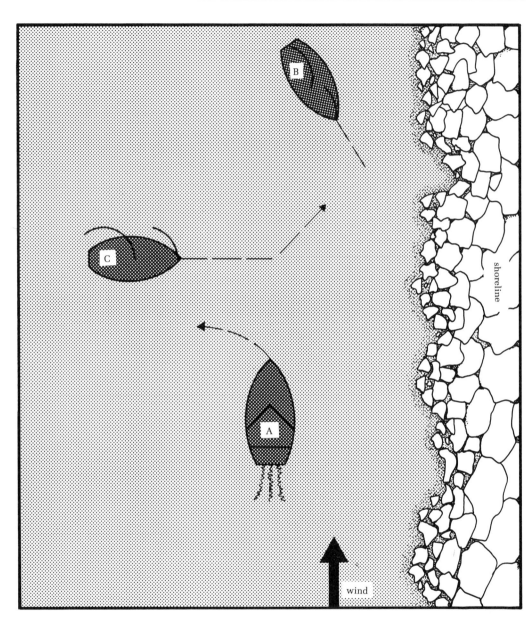

Motor cruiser A with the wind behind would do well to alter course sharply to port as yacht B will soon alter to starboard, on to the port tack, and cross her bows. B will then have to alter course again for yacht C which is on the starboard tack.

Most sailing boats will hoist and lower their sails when heading directly into the wind and at this time it is difficult for them to change course even assuming that they may have their engine running.

The power boat skipper should also be aware of the needs of a sailing boat when she is tacking or beating – that is, sailing close-hauled on alternate tacks – in confined waters. Most sailing boats will tack through about 80 to 90 degrees. That is, they will change direction from having the wind on one side to having it on the other by turning the bows of the boat through the direction from which the wind is coming. So, a power boat travelling along a narrow channel or close to shore with the wind behind and meeting a close-hauled sailing vessel can assume that the sailing vessel will change course towards him through about 90 degrees before reaching the edge of the channel or the shallows. If the power boat skipper understands what the sailing boat is doing he or she will only have to make a minor alteration of course or speed to leave room for the sailing boat to come past on its next tack.

As mentioned earlier and laid down in Rule 25, a vessel under sail that is also being propelled by machinery should show an inverted cone in the fore part of the vessel. This indicates that she is under power and must therefore follow the rules as a power-driven vessel. It is, however, an unfortunate fact that very few vessels while under sail and also under power actually do show this signal. So, while it may seem that a vessel sailing may also be under power, if she is not displaying the appropriate signal she should be treated as a sailing vessel although she is liable to prosecution for not conforming to what is a very specific requirement of the rules.

Rule 13

OVERTAKING

(a) Notwithstanding anything contained in the Rules of part B, sections I and II, any vessel overtaking any other shall keep out of the way of the vessel being overtaken.

(b) A vessel shall be deemed to be overtaking when coming up with another vessel from a direction more than 22.5 degrees abaft her beam, that is, in such a position with reference to the vessel she is overtaking, that at night she would be able to see only the sternlight of that vessel but neither of her sidelights.

(c) When a vessel is in any doubt as to whether she is overtaking another, she shall assume that this is the case and act accordingly.

(d) Any subsequent alteration of the bearing between the two vessels shall not make the overtaking vessel a crossing vessel within the meaning of these Rules or relieve her of the duty of keeping clear of the overtaken vessel until she is finally past and clear.

Discussion on Rule 13

The first part of this rule very clearly points out that whatever the overtaking vessel may be, whether power or sail, towing or fishing it is her responsibility to keep clear of the vessel being overtaken. Having said this, the rule should not be taken to imply that the vessel being overtaken is free to make any course alteration that may bring her into a close-quarters situation with the overtaking vessel. Problems arise when the vessel being overtaken is unaware of the fact that she is being overtaken and makes a course alteration. This highlights the need for all vessels to keep a good all-round lookout as

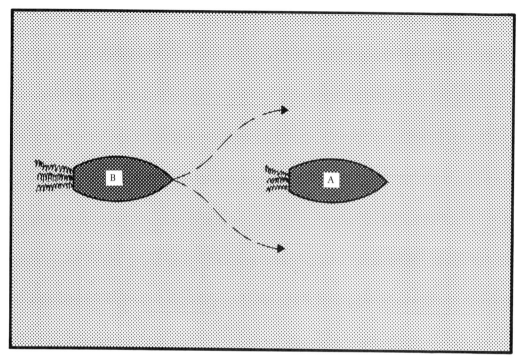

A must hold her course until B is safely past.

discussed with Rule 5. In narrow channels it is common for large vessels to speak to each other over the VHF and ask on which side they should overtake.

It is often the case that a vessel that is about to be overtaken may herself be overtaking a smaller boat that the vessel overtaking her cannot see. She may also be keeping to one side of the channel specifically because she is heading for a berth on that side or is about to slow down and pick up tugs or a pilot.

Once a vessel has become an overtaking vessel through approaching another from any point beyond 22.5 degrees abaft the other's beam, it remains her responsibility to keep clear of the other until she is past and clear. The rule also clearly states that if you are not sure as to whether you are

actually within this overtaking arc then you must assume that you are and act accordingly.

Common sense dictates that the vessel being overtaken should hold as steady a course as possible until the overtaker is well past and clear. If a course change is necessary it should be made well before the overtaking vessel reaches anything like a close-quarters situation, and where possible any alteration should be made so as to avoid crossing close ahead of the other vessel.

This rule highlights the need for care to be taken when altering course in any situation. Many accidents are caused, and many more narrowly avoided, by course changes being made without first determining that there is nothing astern or that

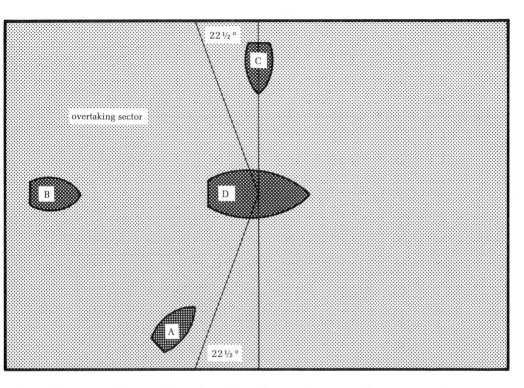

Both A and B are overtaking D and must keep clear of her. So also must C who is not overtaking but has D on her starboard side.

the new course will not conflict with the track of another vessel. The converse can of course also be true in that it is possible that the overtaking vessel may not have seen the vessel that she is overtaking. Most often this will be when a small vessel is being overtaken by one that is much larger, either at night or in bad weather conditions.

In this situation if you feel that you have not been seen then it is probably best to turn so that you are directly stern on to the other vessel. If you feel that you have still not been seen and that there may be a dangerous situation developing it may be as well to fire a white flare. This is also probably one of the few occasions when it may be best to turn to port. If you believe that the other vessel is not taking any or enough action to avoid a collision, turning to port to get out of her way could be the safest thing to do as it should be the natural reaction of the other, when they see you, to turn to starboard.

Rule 14

HEAD-ON SITUATION

(a) When two power-driven vessels are meeting on reciprocal or nearly reciprocal courses so as to involve risk of collision each shall alter her course to starboard so that each shall pass on the port side of the other.

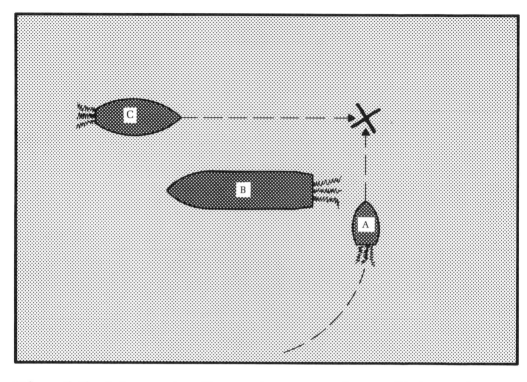

Make sure that by altering course to avoid one vessel you are not putting yourself in danger with another as could be the case here – caused by vessel A passing too close astern of vessel B and therefore not seeing C until the last moment which might be too late.

(b)   Such a situation shall be deemed to exist when a vessel sees the other ahead or nearly ahead and by night she could see the masthead lights of the other in a line or nearly in a line and/or both sidelights and by day she observes the corresponding aspect of the other vessel.

(c)   When a vessel is in any doubt as to whether such a situation exists she shall assume that it does exist and act accordingly.

Discussion on Rule 14

This rule covers the situation that gives rise to more confusion than many others and indeed has been the cause of many collisions and an awful lot of near misses. If the rule is followed properly there will be no problems, but beware the temptation to make do with a slight course alteration. This is the action that most often leads to the development of dangerous close-quarters situations and ultimately almost unavoidable collisions.

Problems usually arise when two vessels approach each other on reciprocal courses that would leave them passing each other starboard side to starboard side with little clearance. Here the temptation is to make a slight course alteration to port to ensure a wider and safer gap. This is the most dangerous move possible. Rule 8 and Rule 16 both require that alterations of

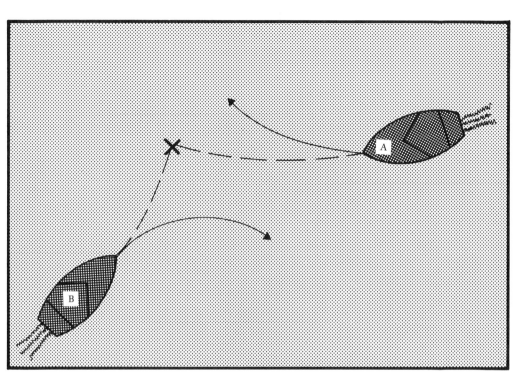

The 'nearly end on situation'. If vessel A makes a slight course alteration to starboard and vessel B does the same to port they will collide. If both follow the rule and alter substantially to starboard they will pass clear 'port to port'.

course that are made in order to avoid the risk of collision should be large enough to be readily apparent. A small course alteration could be interpreted by the other vessel as an indication that the helmsman is half asleep.

If one vessel does make a small alteration of course to port and the other alters, correctly, to starboard it is probable that the first will alter further to port. Panic may then set in on one or other of the vessels and the resultant series of changing courses will, in all probability, end up at best in a near miss or at worst in a collision.

Many power boat skippers think that the instant application of lots of power will take them safely clear of the other. Occasionally this may work, but it is always possible that the other skipper will do likewise and thus totally confuse the whole situation. Increasing speed merely serves to cut down the available thinking time and ensures that any collision that does occur will result in greater damage to all. It is better by far to slow down and give yourself more thinking time.

Rule 15

CROSSING SITUATION

When two power-driven vessels are crossing so as to involve risk of collision, the vessel which has the other on her own

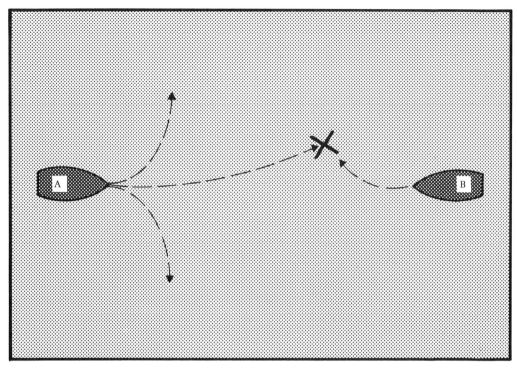

The head-on situation which causes most problems. If A alters slightly to port to avoid being head on she may still collide with B when she correctly alters course to starboard. A should alter to starboard as well but may alter sharply to port well in advance if there are other reasons for not altering to starboard.

starboard side shall keep out of the way and shall, if the circumstances of the case admit, avoid crossing ahead of the other vessel.

Discussion on Rule 15

This rule says that the vessel with the other on her own starboard side should keep out of the way of the other. It does not stipulate what specific action she should take apart from saying that she should avoid crossing ahead of the other.

The safest action to take in most cases is for the give-way vessel to turn to starboard and pass around the stern of the other, making sure to give it a wide berth especially if it is towing or fishing. This follows on from Rule 14. Should the two vessels actually be heading towards each other it then makes no difference whether they are crossing or meeting on something that may be approaching a head-on situation.

There may be occasions where a turn to starboard is not practicable because of other vessels or navigational hazards. Making a claim for a boat written off on the rocks by saying that you altered course to go around the stern of another vessel may not be viewed too sympathetically by your insurance company.

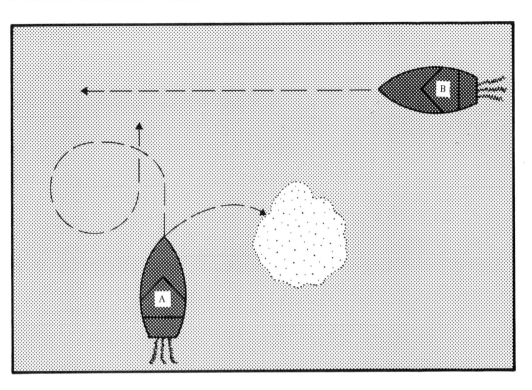

If there is a problem on the starboard side A can make a complete circle to port and then pass astern of B.

If there is a problem about altering to starboard then the course alteration to port should be as sharp as possible to avoid crossing ahead of the other. It may even be best to make a complete circle and thus come up behind the other or on a course that is now parallel to it until it is past. Or, there is the option of slowing down or stopping until the other vessel is well clear. If this latter action is chosen it becomes important to ensure that there is nothing astern before slowing down.

Rule 16

ACTION BY GIVE-WAY VESSEL

Every vessel which is directed to keep out of the way of another vessel shall, so far as possible, take early and substantial action to keep well clear.

Discussion on Rule 16

This rule reiterates the requirements of Rules 8(f) and 10(j). By following this simple edict of taking action early and positively, close-quarters situations are easily avoided and others are left in no doubt as to your intentions.

Rule 17

ACTION BY STAND-ON VESSEL

(a) (i) Where one of two vessels is to

keep out of the way the other shall keep her course and speed.

(ii) The latter vessel may however take action to avoid collision by her man-oeuvre alone, as soon as it becomes apparent to her that the vessel required to keep out of the way is not taking appropriate action in compliance with these Rules.

(b) When, from any cause, the vessel required to keep her course and speed finds herself so close that collision cannot be avoided by the action of the give-way vessel alone, she shall take such action as will best aid to avoid collision.

(c) A power-driven vessel which takes action in a crossing situation in accordance with subparagraph (a)(ii) of this Rule to avoid collision with another power-driven vessel shall, if the circum-stances of the case admit, not alter course to port for a vessel on her own port side.

(d) This Rule does not relieve the give-way vessel of her obligation to keep out of the way.

Discussions on Rule 17

There can be many reasons why a vessel that is supposed to give way to another, according to the requirements of the rules, is unable to do so or is unaware of the need to do so. This rule outlines what the stand-on vessel should, may and must do if she is in doubt as to whether the actions of the other vessel may be too late or insufficient to avoid a collision.

Part (a)(i) clearly states that the stand-on vessel *must* hold her course and speed. Any vessel sighting another needs time to assess where and at what speed the other is heading. If one is wandering around all over the ocean it will make it extremely difficult for the other to decide whether there is the possibility of the two getting close to each other and if so who should give way. In a small boat in heavy weather it may be difficult to hold a really steady course. But if another vessel is sighted the helmsman must be made aware of the need to do his or her best.

Should it become apparent that the vessel that is required to keep clear is not taking the appropriate action then part (a)(ii) says that the stand-on vessel *may* take action to avoid a collision. The problem facing the stand-on vessel is to decide how long to wait before doing something herself. Too late and a collision may occur, too early and she may confuse the other vessel as to her own movements. This situation once again illustrates the need for any action taken to be such that it clearly shows the intention of keeping clear.

Before taking action the stand-on vessel must consider all the circumstances. The other vessel may not be able to alter course as she may be required to by the rules because of other traffic or navigational hazards. She may well be a vessel restric-ted by her draught and unable to alter course whose signals indicating this cannot be seen by the small-boat skipper. Alternatively, she may not have seen the other vessel. This may well be the case when a big ship meets a small boat in heavy weather. A white hull can easily be missed amongst a sea of white-capped waves. Even with sails up it can be difficult to spot a small boat in these circumstances. On the other hand she may have been tracking the other vessel on radar and have decided that there is no need to change course. She may just be leaving it very late or not doing enough to satisfy the stand-on vessel that her action alone will be sufficient to avoid a possible collision. In this latter circumstance, the rule clearly states that the stand-on vessel *shall* take whatever action she feels may be necessary to avoid a collision. If, from a safe distance, you are able to read the name of the larger vessel it may be worth calling her up on VHF to see if she has in fact seen you. If she has plotted you on her radar she may be able to advise whether she feels that you should alter or hold your course.

If the stand-on vessel does decide to make a change in course then she must make one that will keep her clear of the other in the event the other does take the appropriate action at the last minute. So the skipper must decide what that action should be and where he or she must go to stay clear.

By day it is always worthwhile letting the other vessel know that she has been seen. There is nothing more frustrating than seeing a vessel approaching with a number of bodies in the cockpit huddled behind the spray hood and not knowing whether you have been seen. Give a wave, show yourself and scan the other through the binoculars. If the other is a sailing boat you may be in its blind arc. Shout 'starboard' if it is a port and starboard tack situation. If there is no acknowledgement then you may have to assume that you have not been seen or heard and must take action yourself.

By night, of course, there will be no way of telling whether you have been seen or of advising the other vessel that you have seen them. If the situation has developed to the point where you believe there is risk of collision then it could be time to fire a white flare to advise of your presence.

Part (c) of this rule is intended to try to prevent a closing or crossing situation developing should the give-way vessel

subsequently make the correct change of course to starboard to go around your stern after you have taken action. There is always the option of turning back on to your own reciprocal course until the other is clear.

Rule 18

RESPONSIBILITIES BETWEEN VESSELS

Except where Rules 9, 10 and 13 otherwise require:

(a) A power-driven vessel under way shall keep out of the way of:
  (i) a vessel not under command;
  (ii) a vessel restricted in her ability to manoeuvre;
  (iii) a vessel engaged in fishing;
  (iv) a sailing vessel.

(b) A sailing vessel under way shall keep out of the way of:
  (i) a vessel not under command;
  (ii) a vessel restricted in her ability to manoeuvre;
  (iii) a vessel engaged in fishing.

(c) A vessel engaged in fishing when under way shall, so far as possible, keep out of the way of:
  (i) a vessel not under command;
  (ii) a vessel restricted in her ability to manoeuvre.

(d) (i) Any vessel other than a vessel not under command or a vessel restricted in her ability to manoeuvre shall, if the circumstances of the case admit, avoid impeding the safe passage of a vessel constrained by her draught, exhibiting the signals in Rule 28.
  (ii) A vessel constrained by her draught shall navigate with particular caution having full regard to her special condition.

(e) A seaplane on the water shall, in general, keep well clear of all vessels and avoid impeding their navigation. In circumstances, however, where risk of collision exists, she shall comply with the Rules of this part.

Discussion on Rule 18

This rule clearly establishes a pecking order of priorities that is entirely logical and is directly related to the manoeuvrability of the various types of vessels. But the sting is in the beginning where the contents of the rule are prefaced by the statement 'Except where Rules 9, 10 and 13 otherwise require'.

Herein lies the rub and this is largely where the old standard of 'power gives way to sail' is revoked and where 'bigger is better' comes into play. The original concept of power giving way to sail was established when the majority of seagoing sailing vessels were either partially or wholly square-rigged. Vessels rigged this way were incapable of sudden course changes and indeed could only sail to within about 65 degrees of the wind direction. Also, in those days few sailing vessels had any form of auxiliary power to help them along when the wind died or when they wanted to head more directly into the wind. In these circumstances most would anchor and wait for the wind to shift in their favour.

Today, of course, most sailing boats, but not all, do have an auxiliary engine and good seamanship dictates that this should always be ready for use if not actually running when in narrow channels or otherwise enclosed waters. Indeed, many harbour authorities have promulgated their own by-laws which categorically require sailing vessels to use their

Some older yachts – like *Velsheda* seen here – have no engines.

auxiliary engines when in certain areas of their ports. An example of this is at Portsmouth which has a narrow entrance channel and a lot of commercial and Royal Naval traffic. Here, the Queen's Harbour Master has decreed that yachts fitted with engines must use them between the Southsea War Memorial and the Ballast Buoy.

While the small-boat skipper must recognize and adhere to the priorities given by this rule it may well be that those laid down in Rules 9, 10, and 13 that provide the exceptions to Rule 18 will be the most often met with in the course of coastal cruising. In terms of priorities and practicalities the small-boat skipper has to accept that he is out there for pleasure while the larger vessels and the fishermen have a living to earn. Whatever the situation the rules must always be observed, but the small-boat skipper will enjoy his freedom more by staying clear of commercial shipping wherever possible.

The Ferrymen

Many of today's ferries are as big and as fast as some of the transatlantic liners that were household names just a few years ago. They have high standards of facilities and stick to rigid timetables whether they are crossing the Solent from Southampton to Cowes or Lymington to Yarmouth, or crossing the Channel from Poole to the Channel Islands or making the short hop from Dover to Calais.

Their routes and destinations dictate

Some people have a death-wish.

Find your way through this lot!

The two yachts are just leaving the small craft channel to cross astern of the ferry.

that these vessels tend to operate more than others within the waters that are the principal playgrounds of pleasure craft. Certainly this is true of Southampton Water and the Solent where there are an estimated 50,000 small craft, and Poole Harbour and the Channel Islands can safely be classified as having the largest concentrations of small craft around the British Isles.

The captains and officers of the ferries that ply the routes through these congested waters and those that navigate across the busiest shipping lane in the world in the Dover Strait have a special range of problems to contend with. In general they feel that most small-craft skippers do their best to keep out of their way and stick to the rules. They say that while the majority play the game the small

percentage that cause problems are more often than not people that should know better.

Captain Vardy of the British Channel Island Ferries' *Rozel* said that far too often they saw yacht races with start and finish lines too close to or actually within the main deep-water channels. 'The clubs themselves should think of the dangers that the competitiors face,' he said. 'Especially around the Channel Islands where the tides run very fast. Their courses should be laid well clear of the main shipping channels so that competitors never need think about taking a chance and diving across in front of a big ship to gain a few extra yards.'

Captain Vardy also said that there were far too many people, both power and sail, who stuck solidly to the middle of the big-

Berthing the *Rozel* in Poole. Captain Vardy has direct control of the engines from the wing of the bridge.

ship channels. This was well illustrated on entering Poole harbour where there is a specially laid small-craft channel leading up to the entrance and then a further, albeit narrow, small-craft channel to one side of the passage used by the big ferries. More and more authorities are having to consider laying such channels for small craft and it is eminently possible that as conditions become more crowded those that do not use them will be fined or otherwise prosecuted.

Captain John Francis whose nineteen years with Red Funnel has seen him taking their ferries into and out of Cowes, the hub of the yachting world, several times a day believes that the majority of yachtsmen act sensibly. 'Some get carried away when they are racing and think that they have a God-given right to their patch of water,' he said, 'but very often it is the old school that still think that power should always give way to sail that cause problems.'

One problem that is not always instantly obvious within the waters close to yachting centres like Cowes and Lymington are the large numbers of small keelboats that still sail without engines. They can cause congestion when they all leave their berths together and have to struggle to keep to the sides of the channel if the wind is in any way fluky. But here it must be said that their skippers and crews are amongst the most skilled to be found, many of them having built their own boats and sailed them for many years.

Impatience is often the main cause of trouble within narrow channels leading to and from populars harbours. In general terms most small craft travel at 5 or 6 knots in these channels, but there are always the impatient few who push past at greater speeds and then have to cut back into the line when a ferry appears. Most of the time these small craft actually travel too close to each other. It only takes one of them with a deeper keel than the others to run aground and maybe slew across the oncoming line of boats for there to be instant chaos.

Captain John Lloyd at Dover Hoverport.

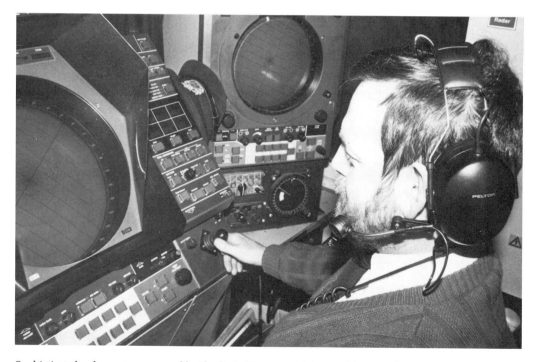

Sophisticated radar systems as used by the first officer on a high-speed hovercraft.

Captain John Lloyd and the skippers of the high-speed hovercraft and catamarans face a very different set of problems. These high-speed craft are being used on more and more routes on both sides of the Channel as well as on the cross-Channel routes themselves. Their very high speeds and the high angles of drift that they can achieve in certain conditions make it all but impossible for a small craft to judge their actual course.

John Lloyd advises that any small craft that can actually see the high-speed craft approaching should hold their course. He said, 'Our captains are highly skilled and work very closely with the first or navigating officer to determine a path through and round any other vessels. Because of the speed at which our craft travel they keep out of the way of everything else on the water. To this end, the first officer is surrounded by a number of very sophisticated radar sets which quickly tell him the precise course and speed of any other vessels in the vicinity. He will advise the captain of these 'targets' and give him a safe course to steer to avoid them. What has to be realized is that at our operating speeds we will close with a slow

moving sailing yacht just two or three minutes after she sees us over the horizon. By that time our captain will already have made his decisions about course alterations, and these may well have had to take into account the movements of a number of other vessels as well. So, if a small yacht suddenly decides to make a radical alteration of course it can give the captain a serious headache.'

Captain Lloyd also suggested that small craft could help themselves by better use of VHF. He pointed out that whether intending to enter the port or not, all craft large and small within 1 mile (1.6km) of Dover harbour entrance are required to listen to Channel 74 and must use this channel to request permission to enter the harbour. Dover harbour, like many others today, displays a set of light signals that indicate whether vessels may enter or not. What is often not understood by the small-craft skipper is that the light signals currently being displayed may not be for him even though he is within 0.75 mile (1.2km) of the entrance. The signal could well be for a hovercraft that will get there before him but is currently 4–5 miles (6.5–8km) away. Listening or calling up

Harbour entrances can be busy places.

The Admiralty Notices to Mariners or the Small Craft Editions of them will advise you of any changes that may affect your passage plans.

the Port Control on the appropriate channel, in this case 74, will ensure that he knows what is happening and can stand clear of any possible danger. This advice holds good for the approach to any port that handles commercial traffic. Not all may have such stringent rules, but the small-craft skipper should consult his or her almanac or pilot book well in advance of his or her approach and make note of any requirements of this type.

Any port that is known to be a ferry terminal should be approached with special caution with a very careful look-out being maintained. It is all too easy to be caught by concentrating all attention on a ferry that is just leaving the harbour and nearly being run down by another that has approached from astern without being seen. Ferry captains do the best they can to give small craft a wide berth, but often their movements are restricted once in approach channels and when close to their berths whether inward or outward bound.

It is always as well to remember that ferries operate two-way traffic. Watching their movements while approaching will often tell when is a good time to slip into the harbour between arrivals and departures.

Section III – Conduct of Vessels in Restricted Visibility

Rule 3 (1) defines restricted visibility as any condition in which visibility is restricted by fog, mist, falling snow, heavy rainstorms, sandstorms or any other similar causes. It does not lay down the actual range at which visibility is said to be restricted as different situations will be seen differently by different vessels.

Annex III of the Rules provides a table of distances over which the sound-signalling apparatus carried by vessels of different sizes should be audible, and this gives some indication of the range of distances that may be regarded as constituting restricted visibility for vessels of various sizes. The annex does also point out that the distance at which any sound apparatus may be heard can vary greatly depending upon the existing weather conditions.

What must be accepted is that visibility of 2 nautical miles will be much more critical for a 250,000 tonne supertanker travelling at 25 knots than it will be for a yacht cruising at 5 knots. The supertanker may have sophisticated radar and plotting systems that allow it to measure very accurately how close it will come to another vessel from some considerable distance off. But the supertanker will require much more time and space to complete a course alteration than would a yacht. A system failure of the radar and plotting systems on a supertanker would therefore be considerably more serious than it would be on a yacht.

This rule is, however, to do with the conduct of vessels in restricted visibility, sound signals being covered in Rule 35. The rule does very specifically state that it shall be followed when *in or near* an area of restricted visibility as it is quite usual at sea to have totally clear visibility in one direction while travelling close to a dense bank of fog or rain in another. The danger of continuing to travel at normal speed in this situation is the possibility of having to give way to or be given way to by a vessel emerging suddenly from the fog bank or rainstorm. Also, fog banks and rain can change direction and move surprisingly quickly to shroud you in gloom where seconds before you were in sunshine.

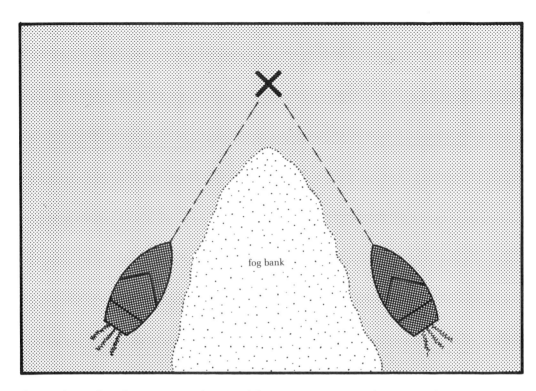

Slowing down when close to an area of poor visibility gives more time to alter course when suddenly confronted by another vessel. Even if you are in a clear patch of a poor visibility area this situation is quite common.

Fog can sweep in very suddenly close inshore or out at sea.

Rule 19

CONDUCT OF VESSELS IN RESTRICTED VISIBILITY

(a) This Rule applies to vessels not in sight of one another when navigating in or near an area of restricted visibility.

(b) Every vessel shall proceed at a safe speed adapted to the prevailing circumstances and conditions of restricted visibility. A power-driven vessel shall have her engines ready for immediate manoeuvre.

(c) Every vessel shall have due regard to the prevailing circumstances and conditions of restricted visibility when complying with the Rules of Section I of this part.

(d) A vessel which detects by radar alone the presence of another vessel shall determine if a close-quarters situation is developing and/or risk of collision exists. If so, she shall take avoiding action in ample time, provided that when such action consists of an alteration of course, so far as possible the following shall be avoided:

(i) an alteration of course to port for a vessel forward of the beam, other than for a vessel being overtaken;

(ii) an alteration of course towards a vessel abeam or abaft the beam.

(e) Except where it has been determined that a risk of collision does not exist, every vessel which hears apparently forward of her beam the fog signal of another vessel, or which cannot avoid a close-quarters situation with another vessel forward of her beam, shall reduce her speed to the minimum at which she can be kept on her course. She shall if necessary take all her way off and in any event navigate with extreme caution until danger of collision is over.

Discussion of Rule 19

Rule 19 essentially requires all vessels to be prepared to take whatever action may be necessary to avoid the risk of collision in conditions of restricted visibility. Sightings will be at close range and there will thus be very little time to make decisions and take appropriate avoiding action.

The rule requires all vessels to travel at a 'safe speed' but does not stipulate what this may be as it will vary from vessel to vessel. What the rule does demand is that engines in a power-driven vessel should be ready for immediate manoeuvre. On large commercial vessels this usually means more people being brought on duty on the bridge and in the engine room where, depending on the kind of propulsion unit installed, there may be special requirements to be met before the engines or the propeller can be slowed, stopped or reversed.

There is a divergence of opinion as to whether a sailing vessel with an auxiliary engine should actually have it running or just tested and ready to start. This must depend on the vessel herself and the individual circumstances. Some sailing boats have very noisy engines and it can be argued that this noise may prevent their crew hearing the other vessel as it approaches, so perhaps in this case it is better to just have it tested and ready to run. Some say that the engine should be running but stopped every couple of minutes to allow the crew to have a good listen out for other vessels. But starting and stopping the engine on a sailing boat eats up battery power which is not usually abundant so this may not be a serious option. However, if the wind is light and the boat barely has steerage way then the best compromise is probably to run the engine and post a listening lookout in the bows where hearing is less likely to be affected by the engine noise.

Sailing boats should also ensure that they are capable of changing course with the minimum of problems when in restricted visibility. It is a popular myth that where there is fog there is little or no wind. This is not always true. Whatever the situation, running free under spinnaker with all of its associated bits and pieces, or indeed sailing under any rig that cannot be handled quickly and easily is not a safe option in fog even with a well-trained crew. A slight hitch getting a spinnaker down or having to let go preventers and so on could spell disaster if the sailing boat is approached suddenly by a large, fast-moving vessel.

Rule 19 also requires all vessels to take heed of the circumstances of restricted visibility when complying with the rules in Section I of the Steering and Sailing Rules (Rules 4 to 10). This of course includes Rule 6 which itself highlights many of the considerations that must be taken into account when judging what may be a safe speed. In a shipping lane or in potentially crowded coastal waters there will obviously be a greater element of danger than there would be if well out to sea or in a more remote coastal area.

In restricted visibility on a small boat without the sophisticated radar systems of the commercial vessels it should be automatic to increase the number of lookouts. The more eyes and ears available the easier it will be to positively identify or dismiss vague shapes or sounds. Many people also get frightened in fog and giving them something positive to do can go some way towards allaying their fears.

Although it can be extremely difficult to

Poor visibility is time for extra lookouts and a radar reflector; some believe in luck.

tell where sounds come from in fog, the rule does suggest that if a fog signal is heard that could be from a vessel that is forward of the beam then speed should be reduced to the absolute minimum that will still give steerage way. It further suggests 'if necessary' the vessel should be stopped. This is a difficult decision to make because it severely limits the ability of the vessel to react to the appearance of another. In a small, high-powered craft steerage way can be attained quickly from a standstill, but a sailing boat or a large, heavy, power-driven vessel will take some time to work up to a speed that will enable it to take any form of evasive action. As it cannot always be guaranteed that the approaching vessel is aware of your

The hand-held fog-horn sounds very loud when you are close to it but it won't be heard at a great distance.

presence, even if you have been making the appropriate sound signals, to actually stop must be a very carefully considered option. Here it must always be remembered that the fog-horns and hooters carried by small boats have a very limited range.

Whatever is decided, once a sound signal has been heard from any quarter the boat should be handled with extreme caution until it is judged that the other is well clear.

If in a small boat you have any warning of a deterioration of visibility and you are in the area of a shipping lane or a narrow channel it makes sense to get out of the lane or to the side of the channel as quickly as possible. Apart from the safety aspect, moving to the side of the channel will ease

your own navigational problems. In poor visibility it will enable you to follow the buoys or other channel markers. In a small-shoal draught boat it may be worth clearing out of the main channel and lying to anchor in the shallows until visibility improves.

Whatever actions you may take with regard to your speed and position relative to traffic lanes, make sure that you are as visible as possible to other vessels by hoisting a radar reflector if you do not have one permanently mounted, and sounding the appropriate fog signals for your own vessel as outlined in Rule 35.

This is a situation where listening in to the conversations of other vessels in the area on VHF can give an indication of the extent of the fog or area of poor visibility.

SUMMARY OF RULES 4–19

- The three sections of Part B, the Steering and Sailing Rules, clearly show what is expected of vessels of all types in both specific and general circumstances.

- You should now understand the importance of keeping a good lookout and how this should be handled in all weathers.

- You should be aware of all of the factors that must be considered with regard to the speed at which you travel.

- How to assess quickly and positively whether risk of collision exists and the criteria that govern any action taken to avoid collision should now be clear in your mind.

- The dangers and specific requirements of navigation within narrow channels and Traffic Separation Schemes have been discussed and described. You should now be able to plan in advance for such areas and ensure that you pass through or across them safely.

- You should know what to do when you are in sight of another vessel and understand the requirements that exist with regard to the priorities between vessels of different types.

- What to do in head-on, crossing and overtaking situations should be understood as should the specific actions required of both the 'give way' and the 'stand on' vessels.

- You should also understand the importance of proper conduct of your vessel in conditions of restricted visibility.

3

RULES FOR LIGHTS AND SHAPES

Rules 20 to 31 describe the specifications and positioning of the lights and shapes that must be exhibited by different types and classes of vessel. Variations of lights and shapes will indicate whether a vessel is going about her normal tasks or whether she may be in circumstances that require her to be treated differently by other vessels – for example, being aground or not under command.

Small-boat owners must ensure that their own lights and shapes comply in every respect with those laid down in these rules for their size and type of vessel. Everyone that may ever be in charge of a small boat must also be able to recognize any and all of the lights and shapes that have to be shown by other vessels. Just by sight of its lights or shapes, you must be able to quickly and accurately assess what kind of vessel it is, what direction it is heading in relation to your own, whether it has right of way and if there are reasons to give it an especially wide clearance.

There are many combinations of colours and configurations and some may seem confusing at first, but they must be learnt. It is no good saying that you do not need to know them because you have no intention of sailing at night. The whims of wind, tide and mechanical failure will soon ensure that you do and then it is no good

saying that you did not intend to be there.

It is very important that the lights on small boats are properly positioned. A stern light is useless if it is covered up by a dingy hung in davits or strapped to the transom, and sidelights that can be seen from either side of the boat will mislead others. The rules lay down very precise angles through which the lights must be visible, and while modern lights are manufactured to comply with these requirements they must be mounted and positioned properly to meet the rules.

Rule 20

APPLICATION
(a)   Rules in this part shall be complied with in all weathers.
(b)   The Rules concerning lights shall be complied with from sunset to sunrise, and during such times no other lights shall be exhibited, except such lights as cannot be mistaken for the lights specified in these Rules or do not impair their visibility or distinctive character, or interfere with the keeping of a proper lookout.
(c)   The lights prescribed by these Rules shall, if carried, also be exhibited from sunrise to sunset in restricted visibility and may be exhibited in all other circumstances when it is deemed necessary.

Stern lights should not be covered. Neither of these could be seen . . .

(d)   The Rules concerning shapes shall be complied with by day.

(e)   The lights and shapes specified in these Rules shall comply with the provisions of Annex I to these Regulations.

Rule 21

DEFINITIONS

(a)   'Masthead light' means a white light placed over the fore and aft centreline of the vessel showing an unbroken light over an arc of the horizon of 225 degrees and so fixed as to show the light from right ahead to 22.5 degrees abaft the beam on either side of the vessel.

(b)   'Sidelights' means a green light on the starboard side and a red light on the port side each showing an unbroken light over an arc of the horizon of 112.5 degrees and so fixed as to show the light from right ahead to 22.5 degrees abaft the beam on its respective side. In a vessel of less than 20 metres in length the sidelights may be combined in one lantern carried on the fore and aft centreline of the vessel.

(c)   'Sternlight' means a white light placed as nearly as practicable at the stern showing an unbroken light over an arc of the horizon of 135 degrees and so fixed as to show the light 67.5 degrees from right aft on each side of the vessel.

(d)   'Towing light' means a yellow light having the same characteristics as the

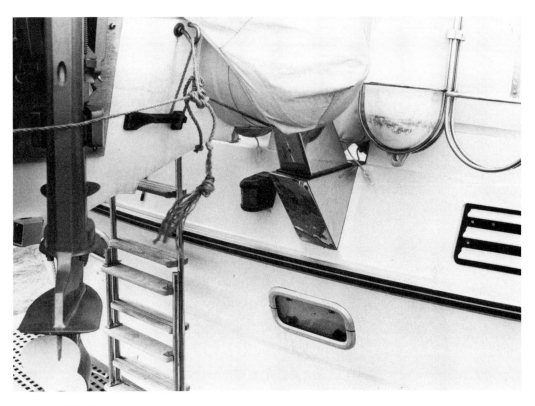

. . . nor could this one.

'sternlight' defined in paragraph (c) of this Rule.

(e) 'All-round light' means a light showing an unbroken light over an arc of the horizon of 360 degrees.

(f) 'Flashing light' means a light flashing at regular intervals at a frequency of 120 flashes or more per minute.

Rule 22

VISIBILITY OF LIGHTS

The lights prescribed in these Rules shall have an intensity as specified in Section 8 of Annex I to these Regulations so as to be visible at the following minimum ranges:

(a) In vessels of 50 metres or more in length:
- a masthead light, 6 miles;
- a sidelight, 3 miles;
- a sternlight, 3 miles;
- a towing light, 3 miles;
- a white, red, green or yellow all-round light, 3 miles.

(b) In vessels of 12 metres or more in length but less than 50 metres in length:
- a masthead light, 5 miles; except that where the length of the vessel is less than 20 metres, 3 miles;
- a sidelight, 2 miles;
- a sternlight, 2 miles;
- a towing light, 2 miles;
- a white, red, green or yellow all-round light, 2 miles.

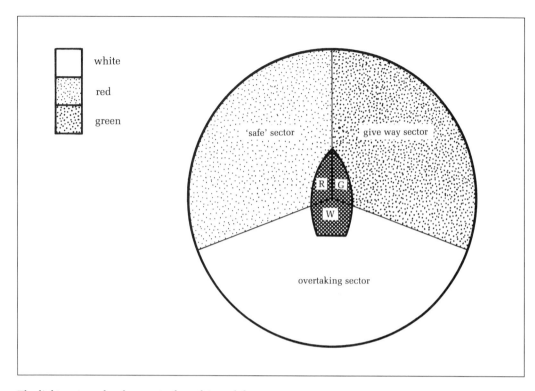

white

red

green

'safe' sector

give way sector

R G

W

overtaking sector

The light sectors also demarcate the safety and danger areas.

(c) In vessels of less than 12 metres in length:
- a masthead light, 2 miles;
- a sidelight, 1 mile;
- a sternlight, 2 miles;
- a towing light, 2 miles;
- a white, red, green or yellow all-round light, 2 miles.

(d) In inconspicuous, partly submerged vessels or objects being towed:
- a white all-round light, 3 miles.

Rule 23

POWER-DRIVEN VESSELS UNDER WAY

(a) A power-driven vessel under way shall exhibit;

(i) a masthead light forward;
(ii) a second masthead light abaft of and higher than the forward one; except that a vessel of less than 50 metres in length shall not be obliged to exhibit such light but may do so;
(iii) sidelights;
(iv) a sternlight.

(b) An air-cushion vessel when operating in the non-displacement mode shall, in addition to the lights prescribed in paragraph (a) of this Rule, exhibit an all-round flashing yellow light.

(c) (i) A power-driven vessel of less than 12 metres in length may in lieu of the lights prescribed in paragraph (a) of this Rule exhibit an all-round white light and sidelights;

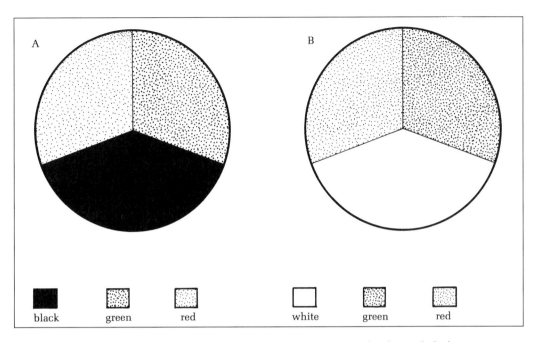

A is a combined bow lantern for vessels of less than 20 metres. B is a masthead or tri-light for yachts of less than 20m (66ft). This must never be used at the same time as the lower navigation lights.

(ii) a power-driven vessel of less than 7 metres in length whose maximum speed does not exceed 7 knots may in lieu of the light prescribed in paragraph (a) of this Rule exhibit an all-round white light and shall, if practicable, also exhibit sidelights;

(iii) the masthead light or all-round white light on a power-driven vessel of less than 12 metres in length may be displaced from the fore and aft centre-line of the vessel if centreline fitting is not practicable, provided that the sidelights are combined in one lantern which shall be carried on the fore and aft centreline of the vessel or located as nearly as practicable in the same fore and aft line as the masthead light or the all-round white light.

Rule 24

TOWING AND PUSHING

(a) A power-driven vessel when towing shall exhibit:

(i) instead of the light prescribed in Rule 23(a)(i) or (a)(ii), two masthead lights in a vertical line. When the length of the tow, measuring from the stern of the towing vessel to the after end of the tow exceeds 200 metres, three such lights in a vertical line;

(ii) sidelights;

(iii) a sternlight;

(iv) a towing light in a vertical line above the sternlight;

(v) when the length of the tow exceeds 200 metres, a diamond shape where it can best be seen.

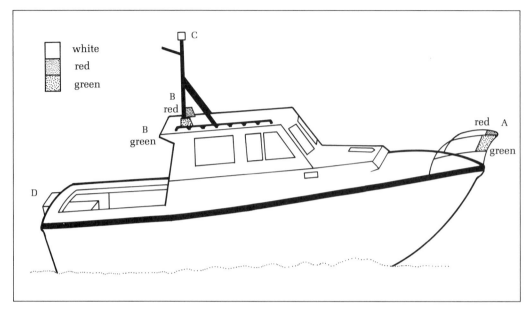

Lights for power craft of under 12m (30ft): A – a combined bow lantern; B – normal sidelights; C – a steaming light; D – a sternlight; C and D may be combined.

(b) When a pushing vessel and a vessel being pushed ahead are rigidly connected in a composite unit they shall be regarded as a power-driven vessel and exhibit the lights prescribed in Rule 23.

(c) A power-driven vessel when pushing ahead or towing alongside, except in the case of a composite unit, shall exhibit;

(i) instead of the light prescribed in Rule 23(a)(i) or (a)(ii), two masthead lights in a vertical line;

(ii) sidelights;

(iii) a sternlight.

(d) A power-driven vessel to which paragraph (a) or (c) of this Rule applies shall also comply with Rule 23(a)(ii).

(e) A vessel or object being towed, other than those mentioned in paragraph (g) of this Rule, shall exhibit:

(i) sidelights;

(ii) a sternlight;

(iii) when the length of the tow exceeds 200 metres, a diamond shape where it can best be seen.

(f) Provided that any number of vessels being towed alongside or pushed in a group shall be lighted as one vessel.

(i) a vessel being pushed ahead, not being part of a composite unit, shall exhibit at the forward end, sidelights;

(ii) a vessel being towed alongside shall exhibit a sternlight and at the forward end, sidelights.

(g) An inconspicuous, partly submerged vessel or object, or combination of such vessels or objects being towed, shall exhibit:

(i) if it is less than 25 metres in breadth, one all-round white light at or near the forward end and one at or near the after end except that dracones need not exhibit a light at or near the forward end;

Easy to identify by day, but would you think of going between barges at night?

(ii)   if it is 25 metres or more in breadth, two additional all-round white lights at or near the extremities of its breadth;

(iii)   if it exceeds 100 metres in length, additional all-round white lights between the lights prescribed in sub-paragraphs (i) and (ii) so that the distance between the lights shall not exceed 100 metres;

(iv)   a diamond shape at or near the aftermost extremity of the last vessel or object being towed and if the length of the tow exceeds 200 metres an additional diamond shape where it can best be seen and located as far forward as is practicable.

(h)   Where from any sufficient cause it is impracticable for a vessel or object being towed to exhibit the light or shapes prescribed in paragraph (e) or (g) of this Rule, all possible measures shall be taken to light the vessel or object towed or at least to indicate the presence of such vessel or object.

(i)   Where from any sufficient cause it is impracticable for a vessel not normally engaged in towing operations to display the lights prescribed in paragraph (a) or (c) of this Rule, such vessel shall not be required to exhibit those lights when engaged in towing another vessel in distress or otherwise in need of assistance. All possible measures shall be taken to indicate the nature of the relationship between the towing vessel and the vessel being towed as authorized by Rule 36, in particular by illuminating the towline.

Rule 25

SAILING VESSELS UNDER WAY
AND VESSELS UNDER OARS

(a)   A sailing vessel under way shall exhibit;

   (i)   sidelights;

   (ii)   a sternlight.

(b)   In a sailing vessel of less than 20

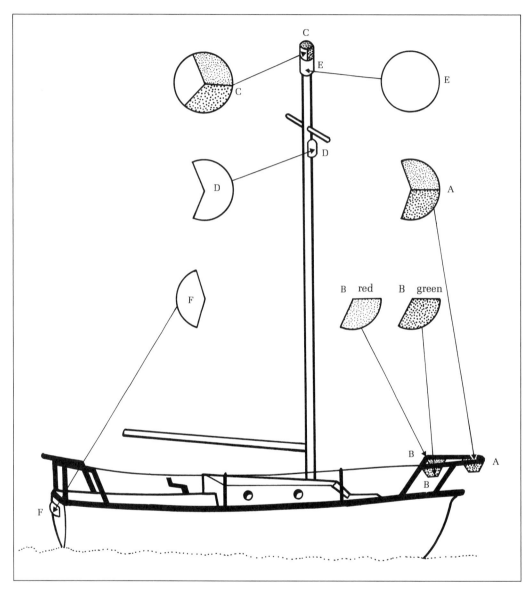

Lights for a sailing craft of under 20m (66ft) can include: A – a combined bow lantern;
B – separate sidelights; C – masthead tri-light; D – a steaming light (for use when under power);
E – an all-round white masthead light to be used as an anchor light or in place of D and F;
F – a sternlight.

metres in length the lights prescribed in paragraph (a) of this Rule may be combined in one lantern carried at or near the top of the mast where it can best be seen.

(c) A sailing vessel under way may, in addition to the lights prescribed in paragraph (a) of this Rule, exhibit at or near the top of the mast, where they can best be seen, two all-round lights in a vertical line, the upper being red and the lower green, but these lights shall not be exhibited in conjunction with the combined lantern permitted by paragraph (b) of this Rule.

(d) (i) A sailing vessel of less than 7 metres in length shall, if practicable, exhibit the lights prescribed in paragraph (a) or (b) of this Rule, but if she does not, she shall have ready at hand an electric torch or lighted lantern showing a white light which shall be exhibited in sufficient time to prevent collision.

(ii) A vessel under oars may exhibit the lights prescribed in this Rule for sailing vessels, but if she does not, she shall have ready at hand an electric torch or lighted lantern showing a white light which shall be exhibited in sufficient time to prevent collision.

(e) A vessel proceeding under sail when also being propelled by machinery shall exhibit forward where it can best be seen a conical shape, apex downwards.

Rule 26

FISHING VESSELS

(a) A vessel engaged in fishing, whether under way or at anchor, shall exhibit only the lights and shapes prescribed in this Rule.

(b) A vessel when engaged in trawling, by which is meant the dragging through the water of a dredge net or other apparatus used as a fishing appliance, shall exhibit:

(i) two all-round lights in a vertical line, the upper being green and the lower white, or a shape consisting of two cones with their apexes together in a vertical line one above the other; a vessel of less than 20 metres in length may instead of this shape exhibit a basket;

(ii) a masthead light abaft of and higher than the all-round green light; a vessel of less than 50 metres in length shall not be obliged to exhibit such a light but may do so;

(iii) when making way through the water, in addition to the lights prescribed in this paragraph, sidelights and a sternlight.

(c) A vessel engaged in fishing, other than trawling shall exhibit:

(i) two all-round lights in a vertical line, the upper being red and the lower white, or a shape consisting of two cones with apexes together in a vertical line one above the other; a vessel of less than 20 metres in length may instead of this shape exhibit a basket;

(ii) when there is outlying gear extending more than 150 metres horizontally from the vessel, an all-round white light or a cone apex upwards in the direction of the gear;

(iii) when making way through the water, in addition to the lights prescribed in this paragraph, sidelights and a sternlight.

(d) A vessel engaged in fishing in close proximity to other vessels engaged in fishing may exhibit the additional signals described in Annex II to these Regulations.

(e) A vessel when not engaged in fishing

shall not exhibit the lights or shapes prescribed in this Rule, but only those prescribed for a vessel of her length.

Rule 27

VESSELS NOT UNDER COMMAND OR RESTRICTED IN THEIR ABILITY TO MANOEUVRE

(a)   A vessel not under command shall exhibit:

(i)   two all-round red lights in a vertical line where they can best be seen;

(ii)   two balls or similar shapes in a vertical line where they can best be seen;

(iii)   when making way through the water, in addition to the lights prescribed in this paragraph, sidelights and a sternlight.

(b)   A vessel restricted in her ability to manoeuvre, except a vessel engaged in mine clearance operations, shall exhibit:

(i)   three all-round lights in a vertical line where they can best be seen. The highest and lowest of these lights shall be red and the middle light shall be white;

(ii)   three shapes in a vertical line where they can best be seen. The highest and lowest of these shapes shall be balls and the middle one a diamond;

(iii)   when making way through the water, a masthead light or lights, sidelights and a sternlight, in addition to the lights prescribed in subparagraph (i);

(iv)   when at anchor, in addition to the lights or shapes prescribed in subparagraphs (i) and (ii), the light, lights or shape prescribed in Rule 30.

(c)   A power-driven vessel engaged in a towing operation such as severely restricts the towing vessel and her tow in their ability to deviate from their course shall,

in addition to the lights or shapes prescribed in Rule 24(a), exhibit the lights or shapes prescribed in subparagraph (b)(i) and (ii) of this Rule.

(d)   A vessel engaged in dredging or underwater operations, when restricted in her ability to manoeuvre, shall exhibit the lights and shapes prescribed in subparagraphs (b)(i), (ii) and (iii) of this Rule and shall in addition, when an obstruction exists, exhibit:

(i)   two all-round red lights or two balls in a vertical line to indicate the side on which the obstruction exists;

(ii)   two all-round green lights or two diamonds in a vertical line to indicate the side on which another vessel may pass;

(iii)   when at anchor, the lights or shapes prescribed in this paragraph instead of the lights or shape prescribed in Rule 30.

(e)   Whenever the size of a vessel engaged in diving operations makes it impracticable to exhibit all lights and shapes prescribed in paragraph (d) of this Rule, the following shall be exhibited:

(i)   three all-round lights in a vertical line where they can best be seen. The highest and lowest of these lights shall be red and the middle light shall be white;

(ii)   a rigid replica of the International Code flag 'A' not less than 1 metre in height. Measures shall be taken to ensure its all-round visibility.

(f)   A vessel engaged in mine clearance operations shall in addition to the lights prescribed for a power-driven vessel in Rule 23 or to the lights or shape prescribed for a vessel at anchor in Rule 30 as appropriate, exhibit three all-round green lights or three balls. One of these lights or shapes shall be exhibited near the fore-

A dredger working in the main channel. Keep well clear as she is very restricted in her ability to manoeuvre.

It is confusing but you can just make out the two diamonds that indicate that you should pass this dredger on her starboard side.

VHF radio communication can solve many problems for the small-boat skipper.

mast head and one at each end of the fore yard. These lights or shapes indicate that it is dangerous for another vessel to approach within 1,000 metres of the mine clearance vessel.

(g) Vessels of less than 12 metres in length, except those engaged in diving operations, shall not be required to exhibit the lights and shapes prescribed in this Rule.

(h) The signals prescribed in this Rule are not signals of vessels in distress and requiring assistance. Such signals are contained in Annex IV to these Regulations.

Rule 28

VESSELS CONSTRAINED BY THEIR DRAUGHT

A vessel constrained by her draught may, in addition to the lights prescribed for power-driven vessels in Rule 23, exhibit where they can best be seen three all-round red lights in a vertical line, or a cylinder.

Rule 29

PILOT VESSELS

(a) A vessel engaged on pilotage duty shall exhibit:

A typical pilot boat with orange superstructure and black hull. At speed they kick up quite a wash.

Both of these ships are at anchor but finding their anchor balls is not easy.

(i)   at or near the masthead, two all-round lights in a vertical line, the upper being white and the lower red;

(ii)   when under way, in addition, sidelights and a sternlight;

(iii)   when at anchor, in addition to the lights prescribed in subparagraph (i), the light, lights or shape prescribed in Rule 30 for vessels at anchor.

(b)   A pilot vessel when not engaged on pilotage duty shall exhibit the lights or shapes prescribed for a similar vessel of her length.

Rule 30

ANCHORED VESSELS AND VESSELS AGROUND

(a)   A vessel at anchor shall exhibit where it can best be seen:

(i)   in the fore part, an all-round white light or one ball;

(ii)   at or near the stern and at a lower level than the light prescribed in subparagraph (i), an all-round white light.

(b)   A vessel of less than 50 metres in length may exhibit an all-round white light where it can best be seen instead of the lights prescribed in paragraph (a) of this Rule.

(c)   A vessel at anchor may, and a vessel of 100 metres and more in length, shall also use the available working or equivalent lights to illuminate her decks.

(d)   A vessel aground shall exhibit the lights prescribed in paragraph (a) or (b) of this Rule and in addition, where they can best be seen:

(i)   two all-round red lights in a vertical line;

(ii)   three balls in a vertical line.

(e)   A vessel of less than 7 metres in length, when at anchor, not in or near a narrow channel, fairway or anchorage, or where other vessels normally navigate, shall not be required to exhibit the lights or shape prescribed in paragraphs (a) and (b) of this Rule.

(f)   A vessel of less than 12 metres in length, when aground, shall not be required to exhibit the lights or shapes prescribed in subparagraphs (d)(i) and (ii) of this Rule.

Rule 31

SEAPLANES

Where it is impracticable for a seaplane to exhibit lights and shapes of the characteristics or in the positions described in the Rules of this part she shall exhibit lights and shapes as closely similar in characteristics and position as is possible.

Discussion on Rules 20 to 31

RULE 20

Rule 20 requires that the lights specified in this section must be shown between sunset and sunrise and in conditions of restricted visibility during normal daylight hours. It is particularly important that small boats show their lights in poor conditions to help the lookouts on other vessels ascertain their size and direction of travel.

In poor visibility it may well be possible to identify the type, size and direction of travel of a big ship as her silhouette will make this more easily apparent. But a lookout on the high bridge of a big ship may have difficulty in determining the course and speed of a small boat that is some distance off and probably travelling relatively slowly. This will be especially true if the wind is above force 5 and there is any kind of sea running. This is not helped by the fact that the predominance of sailing vessels have white hulls and sails that blend in perfectly with waves and spray and which can therefore disappear completely against a background of rain or cloud.

RULE 21

The arcs through which the lights must show as described in Rule 21 are critical. They enable an observer to identify the direction in which a vessel is travelling and to tell when she has made a course alteration that radically changes her bearing or aspect. Buyers of older craft should make sure that whatever navigation lights are fitted do actually comply with the regulations in every way both in angle of visibility and also in range. Many older lights were manufactured to meet now outdated regulations and must be changed.

RULE 22

Rule 22 lays down the minimum ranges of visibility for the various sizes of craft and specific lights with more precise measurements of their actual intensity being laid down in Annex I to the regulations. Unless you happen to be in the business of manufacturing such lights then the figures in Annex I will be of academic interest. What you must do is ensure that your boat is fitted with lights that comply with these regulations.

RULES 23 to 31

Rules 23 to 31 define the lights that shall be shown by vessels of different types and

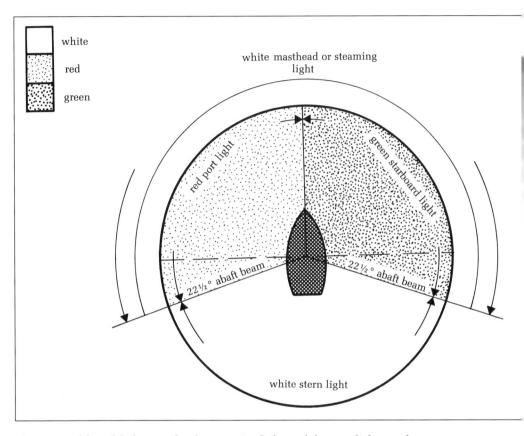

The sectors of the sidelights, masthead or steaming lights and the stern lights are the same for all vessels.

sizes and under varying conditions of activity. The diagrams on the inside covers of this book illustrate some of the potential combinations that may be seen, but it is critically important that the small-boat skipper is able to recognize the majority of lights described in the rules and make a reasonable assessment of what some of the more obscure combinations may mean to him or her.

Dredgers, minesweepers and other naval vessels and fishing fleets can all be very confusing, but what the small-boat skipper needs to be aware of is that it is in his best interests to keep clear of any and all of these. What they are actually doing may not be relevant provided they are given a sufficiently wide berth in a direction that keeps the small boat well clear of their nets, trawls or other outlying equipment. It is an unfortunate fact that not all fishing vessels comply properly with the regulations for lights or shapes by night or day and when they are working their movements can be very erratic. All the more reason to keep well away from them whenever possible.

Under Rule 25, sailing vessels of less

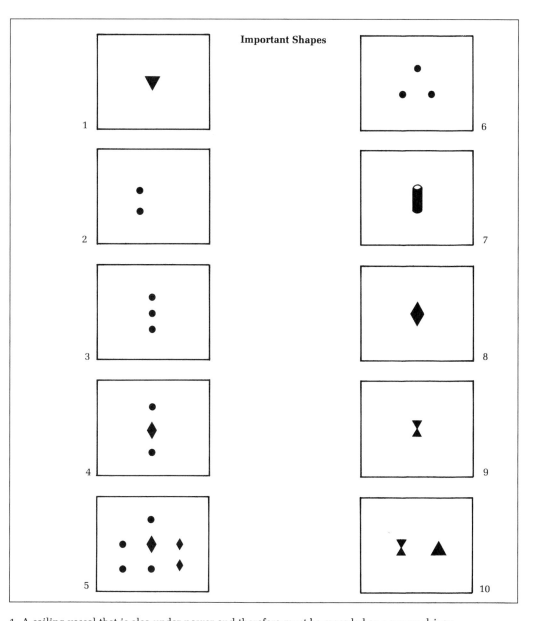

1. A sailing vessel that is also under power and therefore must be regarded as a power driven vessel (Rule 25).   2. A vessel not under command (Rule 27).   3. A vessel aground (Rule 30).
4. A vessel restricted in her ability to manoeuvre (Rule 27).   5. A dredger at work to be passed on the side showing the two diamonds (Rule 27).   6. A minesweeper at work (Rule 27).
7. A vessel constrained by her draught (Rule 28).   8. A vessel towing with a length of tow of more than 200 metres (Rule 24).   9. A vessel engaged in fishing (Rule 26).
10. A vessel engaged in fishing, other than trawling, with gear extending more than 150 metres outwards in the direction of the cone (Rule 26).

Sidelights come in all shapes and sizes. With screens above the superstructure . . .

than 20 metres are allowed to combine sidelights and stern light in a single lantern, usually called a tricolour, at or near the top of the mast as well as having sidelights and stern lights fitted at or near their deck or superstructure level. However, the masthead tricolour lantern must under no circumstance be lit at the same time as the lower navigation lights. The combination will lead to confusion when seen from any angle. It is a simple matter to ensure that this cannot happen, by having both sets of lights on either a rotary or a toggle switch which makes it impossible for both to be on at the same time.

Although there is no rule which states when either upper or lower navigation lights should be used by a sailing vessel, many big-ship captains suggest that yachtsmen should use the lower set of navigation lights when close inshore or

. . . as a combined lantern at the bow . . .

. . . or with screens on the pulpit.

Or the real traditional style.

within busy shipping areas. They believe that this actually makes them more visible as the masthead lights seen from the bridge of a big ship will often get lost amongst the background clutter of shore lights. Use of the lower lights also enables the watching vessel to more accurately assess the distance away that the yacht may be.

When out of busy channels and away from shore then the masthead tricolour is obviously the favourite for yachtsmen as it only requires the power to light one bulb. It is also, in theory, visible from a greater distance being set higher up. If the yacht is under power as well as sail she must carry a steaming light in addition to the side and stern lights. This means that the lower lights only must be used as the rules require the steaming light to be above the level of the sidelights.

The requirement in Rule 25 for a vessel under sail that is also making use of her engine to show a cone forward is probably the least observed of all of the rules. While this is more often than not met merely with despairing looks from British officialdom, yachtsmen motor sailing into Continental ports without displaying the cone may well be met by the harbour master and fined on the spot. This should happen more often in the United Kingdom because the failure to display the cone is usually for no reason other than laziness, and in some cases where the vessel is on the starboard tack it may be a response to the thought of not having to give way to others who may be sailing on the port tack. But overall it is just bad seamanship. It can of course lead to dangerous situations by confusing others when the vessel that is actually motor sailing suddenly changes course in a manner which she would not be able to if she were under sail alone.

These will not show over the proper arcs.

Many small commercial fishing vessels are extremely lax about the lights and shapes which they exhibit, especially those in relation to outlying gear. However, most of them will show the appropriate red and white or green and white all-round lights, so the small-boat skipper seeing these is advised to keep well clear. Passing through a fleet of fishing vessels by night or by day can be a most nerve-wracking experience and the extra mile or two covered to go around the fleet may mean a little time lost but will be much easier on the nerves.

The lights required in Rules 27, 28 and 30 all mean the same to a small boat. Keep clear, because I can not. The requirements of Rule 30 for an anchor ball to be displayed during daylight hours is regrettably another rule that is not always followed by small boats although the majority do tend to use the anchor light at night. While it may be perfectly obvious to other small vessels that you are at anchor it is very difficult for the lookout on a big ship to tell if this is the case. Speed and size differential may make it appear that you are just travelling very slowly. If you are anchored and possibly pointing across the channel, say at the turn of the tide, this may cause the big-ship skipper to take unnecessary avoiding action.

Many people confuse the lights for a pilot vessel as required in Rule 29 with the lights for a vessel fishing as laid down in Rule 27. Here again they must be learnt because the pilot boat when it is not travelling, usually very quickly, from its station to a vessel or vice versa may well be waiting, with a pilot on board, for the arrival of a vessel at a certain point. In this

This committee boat is marking a start or finish line – interesting anchor ball!

situation the pilot boat will probably patrol at slow speed within a small area in much the same manner as a fishing vessel may be expected to, but of course it can be passed reasonably close to as it will not have any outlying gear.

Use of VHF

Often the most difficult aspect of complying with the rules is knowing whether a close-quarters situation is going to develop. This is especially true when visibility is poor and the vessels concerned are some distance apart, or when there is a big difference between the speeds of the two vessels concerned. Although the rules say that if there is any doubt as to whether the risk of collision exists then such risk shall be deemed to exist (Rule 7). But, the doubt can often be cleared away if contact can be made with the other vessel.

Very often this can be achieved by sensible use of VHF. Big-ship captains, port control officers, coastguards and others all feel that small-craft skippers should make more use of VHF in such circumstances. But they also feel generally that there is a need for small-craft skippers as a whole to improve their VHF operating procedures.

Before installing a VHF set the owner should have passed an exam and obtained an Operator's Certificate of Competence. He must also obtain a Ship Licence from the Department of Trade and Industry. This licence allows the set to be used on a specific vessel with an allotted call sign which is not transferable. It is important that correct operating procedures are used because this will keep messages short and ensure that whatever information is required is obtained as quickly as possible. In this way the frequencies are left clear for other users.

If you are approaching a busy port or about to leave from a berth within one then you should be listening to the port control working channel which will be given in the nautical almanac. Many ports make regular broadcasts covering major shipping movements within their areas. Some also require all vessels approaching closer than certain distances to listen on their working channel in case they have to be asked to change course or stop. Listening on the port working channel will often help you decide when and by what route to leave your berth so that you stay clear of any big ship movements. If, however, you have missed a broadcast and must leave by a comparatively narrow channel that is also used by commercial traffic, a call to the port control on one of their working channels will usually give the answers you need. But do be brief, port control radio operators are busy people.

Similarly, if you are in an area where there is radar coverage of a Traffic Separation Scheme which you wish to cross then call the coastguard or TSS control. They will be able to tell you the volume of traffic and may even be able to suggest when there will be a gap in a lane when it will be safe and simple for you to cross. Also, once you have called them they may well keep an eye on you and call you up if they see problems arising.

Out at sea if you can see a name or establish the nationality of a vessel that you feel may come close to you, you can call her on Channel 16. Try various ways of identifying her and yourself, such as: 'large green container ship heading westwards five miles south-west of the Needles fairway buoy this is yacht so and so on your port bow . . . ' But do make sure that you are talking to the correct ship. It is embarrassing to steam ahead and discover that the ship about to run you down because he did not turn to port as expected was not the one you were talking to.

Once you have established contact with another vessel he may advise you to stand on or request that you alter course. This latter request may be to save him a major deviation or problems with other vessels which you cannot see but which he can on his radar. He may also give you his own course and speed.

In or near a narrow channel it can be worth calling a vessel that appears to be heading out of the channel to ascertain where she is heading should this possibly affect you. This is also a place where dual watch on the VHF can be useful so that you can listen in on Channel 16 to contacts being made between other vessels who may be overtaking each other and discussing (briefly) on which side they will pass. This could affect you.

The radio must, however, be used in moderation. The rules have been written to ensure that each vessel clearly understands what is required of her in any given situation. The use of radio should be restricted to those situations where advance warning will make life safer and easier for all. And of course, VHF is the prime means of sending out a Mayday call or advising of other urgent matters with a Pan Pan call or through direct contact with the coastguard. This highlights the very real need to restrict the use of VHF transmissions to urgent messages only, and to ensure that the three-minute silence periods following the hour and the half-hour are complied with rigidly.

SUMMARY OF RULES 20–31

- Knowing what it is that you are looking at can be difficult at sea, especially from the heaving deck or cockpit of a small boat and in poor visibility.

- The lights and shapes described in Rules 20 to 31 are designed to make identification as easy as possible.

- They must be learned by heart.

- You must know what another vessel is, how she is heading and whether she is in any way restricted in her movements, before you can make any decisions with regard to your own actions.

- You must know what lights and signals you must show on your own vessel in any given situation.

- You should be able to make a reasonable assessment of what any set of lights might be, given the circumstances under which you see them – you may be seeing the lights of a number of vessels that are close to each other or a mix of lights from ships and shore. Being aware of where you are and what is happening around you will often supply the clues.

4

SOUND AND LIGHT SIGNALS

Rules 32 to 36 cover the sound and light signals that must be given by vessels of varying types as warnings, to attract attention, to denote specific manoeuvres and to denote their presence and activity in conditions of restricted visibility.

The specifications for sound-signalling equipment for vessels of various sizes are laid down in Annex III to the rules, and while they are really only of academic interest to the small-boat owner they should be read to give a grasp of what is expected in terms of range of audibility and basic characteristics.

Rule 32

DEFINITIONS

(a)   The word 'whistle' means any sound-signalling appliance capable of producing the prescribed blasts and which complies with the specifications in Annex III to these Regulations.

(b)   The term 'short blast' means a blast of about one second's duration.

(c)   The term 'prolonged blast' means a blast of from four to six seconds' duration.

Rule 33

EQUIPMENT FOR SOUND SIGNALS

(a)   A vessel of 12 metres or more in length shall be provided with a whistle and a bell and a vessel of 100 metres or more in length shall, in addition, be provided with a gong, the tone and sound of which cannot be confused with that of the bell. The whistle, bell and gong shall comply with the specifications in Annex III to these Regulations. The bell or gong or both may be replaced by other equipment having the same respective sound characteristics, provided that manual sounding of the prescribed signals shall always be possible.

(b)   A vessel of less than 12 metres in length shall not be obliged to carry the sound-signalling appliances prescribed in paragraph (a) of this Rule but if she does not, shall be provided with some other means of making an efficient sound signal.

Rule 34

MANOEUVRING AND WARNING SIGNALS

(a)   When vessels are in sight of one another, a power-driven vessel under way,

A good set of horns.

when manoeuvring as authorized or required by these Rules, shall indicate that manoeuvre by the following signals on her whistle:

   – one short blast to mean 'I am altering my course to starboard';

   – two short blasts to mean 'I am altering my course to port';

   – three short blasts to mean 'I am operating astern propulsion'.

(b) Any vessel may supplement the whistle signals prescribed in paragraph (a) of this Rule by light signals, repeated as appropriate, whilst the manoeuvre is being carried out:

   (i) these light signals shall have the following significance:

   – one flash to mean 'I am altering my course to starboard';

   –two flashes to mean 'I am altering my course to port';

   – three flashes to mean 'I am operating astern propulsion';

(ii) the duration of each flash shall be about one second, the interval between successive signals shall be not less than ten seconds;

(iii) the light used for this signal shall, if fitted, be an all-round white light, visible at a minimum range of 5 miles, and shall comply with the provisions of Annex I to these Regulations.

(c) When in sight of one another in a narrow channel or fairway:

Moving slowly, this ship with tugs alongside will be making for a berth and will possibly deviate from the main channel. She may use sound signals to indicate her intentions.

(i) a vessel intending to overtake another shall in compliance with Rule 9(e)(i) indicate her intention by the following signals on her whistle:

– two prolonged blasts followed by one short blast to mean 'I intend to overtake you on your starboard side';

– two prolonged blasts followed by two short blasts to mean 'I intend to overtake you on your port side'.

(ii) the vessel about the be overtaken when acting in accordance with Rule 9(e)(i) shall indicate her agreement by the following signal on her whistle:

– one prolonged, one short, one prolonged and one short blast, in that order.

(d) When vessels in sight of one another are approaching each other and from any cause either vessel fails to understand the intentions or actions of the other, or is in doubt whether sufficient action is being taken by the other to avoid collision, the vessel in doubt shall immediately indicate such doubt by giving at least five short and rapid blasts on the whistle. Such signal may be supplemented by a light signal of at least five short and rapid flashes.

(e) A vessel nearing a bend or an area of a channel or fairway where other vessels may be obscured by an intervening obstruction shall sound one prolonged blast. Such signal shall be answered with a

Have a thought for the ferry skipper – somebody just got five blasts.

prolonged blast by any approaching vessel that may be within hearing around the bend or behind the intervening obstruction.

(f) If whistles are fitted on a vessel at a distance apart of more than 100 metres, one whistle only shall be used for giving manoeuvring and warning signals.

Rule 35

SOUND SIGNALS IN RESTRICTED VISIBILITY

In or near an area of restricted visibility, whether by day or night, the signals prescribed in this Rule shall be used as follows:

(a) A power-driven vessel making way through the water shall sound at intervals of not more than 2 minutes one prolonged blast.

(b) A power-driven vessel under way but stopped and making no way through the water shall sound at intervals of not more than 2 minutes two prolonged blasts in succession with an interval of about 2 seconds between them.

(c) A vessel not under command, a vessel restricted in her ability to manoeuvre, a vessel constrained by her draught, a sailing vessel, a vessel engaged in fishing and a vessel engaged in towing or pushing another vessel shall, instead of the signals prescribed in paragraphs (a) or (b) of this Rule, sound at intervals of not more than 2 minutes three blasts in succession, namely one prolonged followed by two short blasts.

(d) A vessel engaged in fishing, when at anchor, and a vessel restricted in her ability to manoeuvre when carrying out her work at anchor, shall instead of the signals prescribed in paragraph (g) of this Rule sound the signal prescribed in paragraph (c) of this Rule.

113

(e)   A vessel towed or if more than one vessel is towed the last vessel of the tow, if manned, shall at intervals of not more than 2 minutes sound four blasts in succession, namely one prolonged followed by three short blasts. When practicable, this shall be made immediately after the signal made by the towing vessel.

(f)   When a pushed vessel and a vessel being pushed ahead are rigidly connected in a composite unit they shall be regarded as a power-driven vessel and shall give the signals prescribed in paragraphs (a) or (b) of this Rule.

(g)   A vessel at anchor shall at intervals of not more than one minute ring the bell rapidly for about 5 seconds. In a vessel of 100 metres or more in length the bell shall be sounded in the forepart of the vessel and immediately after the ringing of the bell the gong shall be sounded rapidly for about 5 seconds in the after part of the vessel. A vessel at anchor may in addition sound three blasts in succession, namely one short, one prolonged and one short blast, to give warning of her position and of the possibility of collision to an approaching vessel.

(h)   A vessel aground shall give the bell signal and if required the gong signal prescribed in paragraph (g) of this Rule and shall, in addition, give three separate and distinct strokes on the bell immediately before and after the rapid ringing of the bell. A vessel aground may in addition sound an appropriate whistle signal.

(i)   A vessel of less than 12 metres in length shall not be obliged to give the above-mentioned signals but, if she does not, shall make some other efficient sound signal at intervals of not more than 2 minutes.

(j)   A pilot vessel when engaged on pilotage duty may in addition to the signals prescribed in paragraphs (a), (b) or (g) of the Rule sound an identity signal consisting of four short blasts.

Rule 36

SIGNALS TO ATTRACT ATTENTION

If necessary to attract the attention of another vessel any vessel may make light or sound signals that can not be mistaken for any signal authorized elsewhere in these Rules, or may direct the beam of her searchlight in the direction of the danger, in such a way as not to embarrass any vessel. Any light to attract the attention of another vessel shall be such that it can not be mistaken for any aid to navigation. For the purpose of this Rule the use of high intensity intermittent or revolving lights, such as strobe lights, shall be avoided.

Discussion on Rules 32 to 36

Rule 33 allows vessels of less than 12 metres a degree of flexibility with regard to the type of sound equipment which they must carry. While most small power boats are fitted with reasonably powerful air-horns, the majority of small yachts tend to carry the hand-held aerosol type of foghorn. While these may not be audible over great ranges, being portable they can be used from the foredeck of a small boat where they will not effectively deafen the rest of the crew in the cockpit. The small brass ship's bell that many yachts carry more as an ornament than anything else may well be put to good use if the vessel has to anchor anywhere near a busy channel or waterway. The high-pitched sound that it emits will stand out well from much other background noise.

Manoeuvring and warning signals are

usually taken to be the province of the big ships but there is no reason why they should not be used in difficult situations by a small vessel. If every small boat in a crowded area like the Solent gave sound signals every time it changed course life would be extremely complicated for everyone. But used with discretion by a small vessel the manoeuvring and warning signals can help eliminate potential close-quarters situations before they arise.

Of the most commonly used manoeuvring and warning signals, the three short blasts which signify that a vessel is operating astern propulsion are often thought to mean that she is actually travelling astern – this is not always the case.

While small-boat owners may not themselves want to use the overtaking signals, it is important that they do understand what they are as they may mean having to vacate or at least keep well to the side of a narrow channel if one large vessel is about to overtake another.

Knowing the meaning of the sound signals designated for use in restricted visibility will ensure that they cannot be mistaken for any fog signals given by lighthouses or other navigational features. Some high-speed vessels such as hovercraft and catamarans do not always sound their fog signals. This is because at speed their propulsion units can be heard at a far greater distance than would their fog signals. Operating at high speed they will be using very sophisticated radar to thread their way through any traffic, whether it is moving or stationary, and actually prefer others to hold their course and speeds.

Attracting the attention of another vessel as described in Rule 36 will most probably happen at night for a small vessel. Typically it will be in a shipping channel where she is in doubt as to whether she has been seen by another larger vessel. Here the small-boat skipper can shine a light on his or her sails, let off a white flare or shine a powerful beamed light in the direction of the other vessel. In any of these cases care must be taken not to blind the occupants of the other vessel, and if using a white flare the small-boat skipper must try to avoid blinding himself or herself or the crew. Night sight takes some time to recover after the eyes have been exposed to bright white light and during the recovery period other objects or vessels may not be seen.

Rule 37

DISTRESS SIGNALS
When a vessel is in distress and requires assistance she shall use or exhibit the signals described in Annex IV to these Regulations.

Discussion on Rule 37

Every small boat should be equipped with a variety of means to alert others to a distress situation. Annex IV sets out the complete list of signals that can be used to attract attention. However, it must be remembered that these signals are only to be used in genuine cases of distress. Probably the most important amongst the signals listed are flares and VHF radio.

Flares can be bought individually or in ready-made-up sets. They have a nominal life of three years after which they should be replaced, although the old ones may be kept on board as extras. For general coastal work a set of distress flares should include at least two red hand-held flares, two red parachute rocket flares and two orange smoke canisters or hand-held flares. There are also many small personal flare systems available that can be carried in a pocket or kept in a small cockpit locker. These will not have a great range of visibility but are better than nothing and are especially worth carrying on your person if you are using a dinghy at night to return to a boat in an anchorage.

Remember, white flares are *not* distress signals, they are used to indicate your presence or position to other vessels. They are commonly called Steamer Scarers.

Every person on board a small boat should know where the flares are kept and how to operate them. They are best kept in a watertight container which will float, along with other emergency items such as a flashlight and first-aid kit. Ideally this should be handy to the cockpit so that if abandoning ship it is close to hand.

The correct procedure for sending a Mayday message by VHF should be known. It is a requirement for the attainment of a radio licence that you can send and understand fully the requirements and content of a Mayday message. If possible an example message should be stuck to the bulkhead adjacent to the VHF so that less experienced crew members can make the broadcast should the skipper or others be incapacitated.

EPIRBs are essentially for the use of the ocean-going or offshore sailor, but where they are carried they must be kept where they can not be accidentally triggered. Once set off these units send out a continuous automatic signal that will be tracked by aircraft or satellite. This will activate a truly international procedure that could involve land, sea and air forces. Having a lifeboat or helicopter arrive as you are tucking in to dinner at a peaceful anchorage may be embarrassing. They will not be pleased to find a junior member of crew has triggered the EPIRB without knowing it or telling you.

SUMMARY OF RULES 32–37

- Every mariner must be familiar with all of the sound and light signals described in Rules 32 to 37 if he is to conduct a vessel in safety within sight or sound of others by night or day.

- These signals tell you what another vessel is doing, or is about to do, and may well have a direct effect on your own actions.

- Sound and light signals are not just the province of the big ships – small craft could well make more use of them to indicate their intentions to others, especially in crowded or narrow waters.

- Fog or poor visibility is always a hazard but a thorough knowledge of the sound signals required for your own and other vessels will enable you to assess what other vessels are in the vicinity and what they are doing.

- Apart from the signals described in Rule 36, which are purely to attract attention, you must also learn all the sound, light and radio signals that can be used to signify distress, as laid out in Annex IV, so that you can quickly identify them if seen and, also, so that you can use them to best advantage yourself should the occasion ever arise.

5

EXEMPTIONS

These exemptions are of little significance to small-craft owners, but once again they show that at night some configurations of lights may not always be exactly what was expected although the variations as seen will probably be hardly perceptible.

Rule 38

EXEMPTIONS

Any vessel (or class of vessels) provided that she complies with the requirements of the International Regulations for Preventing Collisions at Sea, 1960, the keel of which is laid or which is at a corresponding stage of construction before the entry into force of these Regulations may be exempted from compliance therewith as follows:

(a)   The installation of lights with ranges prescribed in Rule 22, until four years after the date of entry into force of these Regulations.

(b)   The installations of lights with colour specifications as prescribed in Section 7 of Annex I to these Regulations, until four years after the date of entry into force of these Regulations.

(c)   The repositioning of lights as a result of conversion from imperial to metric units and rounding off measurement figures, permanent exemption.

(d)   (i)   The repositioning of masthead lights on vessels of less than 150 metres in length, resulting from the prescriptions of Section 3(a) of Annex I to these Regulations, permanent exemption.

(ii)   The repositioning of masthead lights on vessels of 150 metres or more in length, resulting from the prescriptions of Section 3(a) of Annex I to these Regulations, until nine years after the date of entry into force of these Regulations.

(e)   The repositioning of masthead lights resulting from the prescriptions of Section 2(b) of Annex I to these Regulations, until nine years after the date of entry into force of these Regulations.

(f)   The repositioning of sidelights resulting from the prescriptions of sections 2(g) and 3(b) of Annex I to these Regulations, until nine years after the date of entry into force of these Regulations.

(g)   The requirements for sound-signal appliances prescribed in Annex III to these Regulations, until nine years after the date of entry into force of these Regulations.

(h)   The repositioning of all-round lights resulting from the prescription of Section 9(b) of Annex I to these Regulations, permanent exemption.

6
SUMMARY

- The Regulations for Preventing Collisions at Sea have evolved over many years to provide a common code for all seafarers, whether they are in big ships or small boats. There will, of course, always be those few that choose to ignore them or who are just plain ignorant, and that is when the responsible seafarer's judgement and good seamanship come into play.

- Remember Rule 17. There is no point in saying, 'But he should have given way to me!' when you are in the water with bits of your boat around you.

- See and be seen, know what to do and what to expect of others, and you should avoid the danger of collision. Going to sea in a small boat is one of the last real freedoms left, but to enjoy the freedom you must play by the rules.

Going to sea should be a safe and enjoyable experience for all seafarers, whether they are in big ships or small craft.

7
ANNEX I
Positioning and Technical Details of Lights and Shapes

Introduction

Unless you are building your own boat from scratch your vessel will have had its lights fitted by the builders in a manner that should meet with the requirements and specifications laid down in this annex to the rules. If, however, you have purchased an elderly craft it will be as well to check carefully that the lights themselves meet present-day requirements. They also need to be fitted in positions that allow them to shine through the arcs, relative to the centreline of the boat, that are laid down in the rules.

Badly positioned lights, especially sidelights, can give a false impression of your heading and lead to dangerous situations.

1. Definition

The term 'height above the hull' means height above the uppermost continuous deck. This height shall be measured from the position vertically beneath the location of the light.

2. Vertical positioning and spacing of lights

(a) On a power-driven vessel of 20 metres or more in length the masthead lights shall be placed as follows:

(i) the forward masthead light, or if only one masthead light is carried, then that light, at a height above the hull of not less than 6 metres, and, if the breadth of the vessel exceeds 6 metres, then at a height above the hull not less than such breadth, so however that the light need not be placed at a greater height above the hull than 12 metres;

(ii) when two masthead lights are carried the after one shall be at least 4.5 metres vertically higher than the forward one.

(b) The vertical separation of masthead lights of power-driven vessels shall be such that in all normal conditions of trim the after light will be seen over and separate from the forward light at a distance of 1,000 metres from the stem when viewed from sea level.

(c) The masthead light of a power-driven vessel of 12 metres but less than 20 metres in length shall be placed at a height above the gunwale of not less than 2.5 metres.

(d) A power-driven vessel of less than 12 metres in length may carry the uppermost light at a height of less than 2.5 metres above the gunwale. When, however, a masthead light is carried in addition to sidelights and a sternlight or the all-round light prescribed in Rule 23(c)(i) is carried in addition to sidelights, then such masthead light or all-round light shall be carried at least 1 metre higher than the sidelights.

(e)   One of the two or three masthead lights prescribed for a power-driven vessel when engaged in towing or pushing another vessel shall be placed in the same position as either the forward masthead light or the after masthead light; provided that, if carried on the aftermast, the lowest after masthead light shall be at least 4.5 metres vertically higher than the forward masthead light.

(f)   (i) The masthead light or lights prescribed in Rule 23(a) shall be so placed as to be above and clear of all other lights and obstructions except as described in subparagraph (ii).

(ii)   When it is impracticable to carry the all-round lights prescribed by Rule 27(b)(i) or Rule 28 below the masthead lights, they may be carried above the after masthead light(s) or vertically in between the forward masthead light(s) and after masthead light(s), provided that in the latter case the requirement of section 3(c) of this Annex shall be complied with.

(g)   The sidelights of a power-driven vessel shall be placed at a height above the hull not greater than three-quarters of that of the forward masthead light. They shall not be so low as to be interfered with by deck lights.

(h)   The sidelights, if in a combined lantern and carried on a power-driven vessel of less than 20 metres in length, shall be placed not less than 1 metre below the masthead light.

(i)   When the Rules prescribe two or three lights to be carried in a vertical line, they shall be spaced as follows:

(i)   on a vessel of 20 metres in length or more such lights shall be spaced not less

than 2 metres apart, and the lowest of these lights shall, except where a towing light is required, be placed at a height of not less than 4 metres above the hull;

(ii)   on a vessel of less than 20 metres in length such lights shall be spaced not less than 1 metre apart and the lowest of these lights shall, except where a towing light is required, be placed at a height of not less than 2 metres above the gunwale;

(iii)   when three lights are carried they shall be equally spaced.

(j)   The lower of the two all-round lights prescribed for a vessel when engaged in fishing shall be at a height above the sidelights not less than twice the distance between the two vertical lights.

(k)   The forward anchor lights prescribed in Rule 30(a)(i), when two are carried, shall not be less than 4.5 metres above the after one. On a vessel of 50 metres or more in length this forward anchor light shall be placed at a height of not less than 6 metres above the hull.

3.   Horizontal positioning and spacing of lights

(a)   When two masthead lights are prescribed for a power-driven vessel, the horizontal distance between them shall not be less than one half of the length of the vessel but need not be more than 100 metres. The forward light shall be placed not more than one quarter of the length of the vessel from the stem.

(b)   On a power-driven vessel of 20 metres or more in length the sidelights shall not be placed in front of the forward masthead lights. They shall be placed at or near the side of the vessel.

(c)   When the lights prescribed in Rule

23(b)(i) or Rule 28 are placed vertically between the forward masthead light(s) and the after masthead light(s) these all-round lights shall be placed at a horizontal distance of not less than 2 metres from the fore and aft centreline of the vessel in the athwartship direction.

4. Details of location of direction-indicating lights for fishing vessels, dredgers and vessels engaged in under-water operations

(a) The light indicating the direction of the outlying gear from a vessel engaged in fishing as prescribed in Rule 26(c)(ii) shall be placed at a horizontal distance of not less than 2 metres and not more than 6 metres away from the two all-round red and white lights. This light shall be placed not higher than the all-round white light prescribed in Rule 26(c)(i) and not lower than the sidelights.

(b) The lights and shapes on a vessel engaged in dredging or underwater operations to indicate the obstructed side and/or the side on which it is safe to pass, as prescribed in Rule 27(d)(i) and (ii), shall be placed at the maximum practical horizontal distance, but in no case less than 2 metres, from the lights or shapes prescribed in Rule 27(b)(i) and (ii). In no case shall the upper of these lights or shapes be at a greater height than the lower of the three lights or shapes prescribed in Rule 27(b)(i) and (ii).

5. Screens for sidelights

The sidelights of vessels of 20 metres or more in length shall be fitted with inboard screens painted matt black, and meeting the requirements of Section 9 of this Annex. On vessels of less than 20 metres in length the sidelights, if necessary to meet the requirements of Section 9 of this Annex, shall be fitted with inboard matt black screens. With a combined lantern, using a single vertical filament and a very narrow division between the green and red sections, external screens need not be fitted.

6. Shapes

(a) Shapes shall be black and of the following sizes:
    (i) a ball shall have a diameter of not less than 0.6 metre;
    (ii) a cone shall have a base diameter of not less than 0.6 metre and a height equal to its diameter;
    (iii) a cylinder shall have a diameter of at least 0.6 metre and a height of twice its diameter;
    (iv) a diamond shape shall consist of two cones as defined in (ii) above having a common base.
(b) The vertical distance between shapes shall be at least 1.5 metres.
(c) In a vessel of less than 20 metres in length shapes of lesser dimensions but commensurate with the size of the vessel may be used and the distance apart may be correspondingly reduced.

7. Colour specification of lights

The chromaticity of all navigation lights shall conform to the following standards, which lie within the boundaries of the area of the diagram specified for each colour by the International Commission on Illumination (CIE).

The boundaries of the area for each colour are given by indicating the corner co-ordinates, which are as follows:

(i) White

x	0.525	0.525	0.452	0.310	0.443
y	0.382	0.440	0.440	0.348	0.382

(ii) Green

x	0.028	0.009	0.300	0.203
y	0.385	0.723	0.511	0.356

(iii) Red

x	0.680	0.660	0.735	0.721
y	0.320	0.320	0.265	0.259

(iv) Yellow

x	0.612	0.618	0.575	0.575
y	0.382	0.382	0.425	0.406

8. Intensity of lights

(a) The minimum luminous intensity of lights shall be calculated by using the formula:

$$I = 3.43 \times 10^6 \times T \times D^2 \times K^{-D}$$

where

I   is luminous intensity in candelas under service conditions,

T   is threshold factor 2×10^{-7} lux,

D   is range of visibility (luminous range) of the light in nautical miles,

K   is atmospheric transmissivity.

For prescribed lights the value of K shall be 0.8, corresponding to a meteorological visibility of approximately 13 nautical miles.

(b) A selection of figures derived from the formula is given in the following table:

NOTE *The maximum luminous intensity of navigation lights should be limited to avoid undue glare. This shall not be achieved by a variable control of the luminous intensity.*

9. Horizontal sectors

(a) (i) In the forward direction, sidelights as fitted on the vessel shall show the minimum required intensities. The intensities shall decrease to reach practical cut-off between 1 degree and 3 degrees outside the prescribed sectors.

(ii) For sternlights and masthead lights at 22.5 degrees abaft the beam for sidelights, the minimum required intensities shall be maintained over the arc of the horizon up to 5 degrees within the limits of the sectors prescribed in Rule 21. From 5 degrees within the prescribed sectors the intensity may decrease by 50 per cent up to the

Range of visibility (luminous range) of light in nautical miles D	Luminous intensity light in candelas K = 0.8 I
1	0.9
2	4.3
3	12
4	27
5	52
6	94

prescribed limits; it shall decrease steadily to reach practical cut-off at not more than 5 degrees outside the prescribed sectors.

(b) All-round lights shall be so located as not to be obscured by masts, topmasts or structures within angular sectors of more than 6 degrees, except anchor lights prescribed in Rule 30, which need not be placed at an impracticable height above the hull.

10. Vertical sectors

(a) The vertical sectors of electric lights as fitted, with the exception of lights on sailing vessels under way shall ensure that:

(i) at least the required minimum intensity is maintained at all angles from 5 degrees above to 5 degrees below the horizontal;

(ii) at least 60 per cent of the required minimum intensity is maintained from 7.5 degrees above to 7.5 degrees below the horizontal.

(b) In the case of sailing vessels under way the vertical sectors of electric lights as fitted shall ensure that:

(i) at least the required minimum intensity is maintained at all angles from 5 degrees above to 5 degrees below the horizontal;

(ii) at least 50 per cent of the required minimum intensity is maintained from 25 degrees above to 25 degrees below the horizontal.

(c) In the case of lights other than electric these specifications shall be met as closely as possible.

11. Intensity of non-electric lights

Non-electric lights shall so far as practicable comply with the minimum intensities, as specified in the table given in Section 8 of this Annex.

12. Manoeuvring light

Notwithstanding the provisions of paragraph 2(f) of this Annex the manoeuvring light described in Rule 34(b) shall be placed in the same fore and aft vertical plane as the masthead light or lights and, where practicable, at a minimum height of 2 metres vertically above the forward masthead light, provided that it shall be carried not less than 2 metres vertically above or below the after masthead light. On a vessel where only one masthead light is carried the manoeuvring light, if fitted, shall be carried where it can best be seen, not less than 2 metres vertically apart from the masthead light.

13. Approval

The construction of lights and shapes and the installation of lights on board the vessel shall be to the satisfaction of the appropriate authority of the State whose flag the vessel is entitled to fly.

8

ANNEX II

Additional Signals for Fishing Vessels Fishing in Close Proximity

1. General

The lights mentioned herein shall, if exhibited in pursuance of Rule 26(d), be placed where they can best be seen. They shall be at least 0.9 metre apart but at a lower level than lights prescribed in Rule 26(b)(i) and (c)(i). The lights shall be visible all round the horizon at a distance of at least 1 mile but at a lesser distance than the lights prescribed by these Rules for fishing vessels.

2. Signals for trawlers

(a) Vessels when engaged in trawling, whether using demersal or pelagic gear, may exhibit:
    (i)   when shooting their nets: two white lights in a vertical line;
    (ii)   when hauling their nets: one white light over one red light in a vertical line;
    (iii)   when the net has come fast upon an obstruction: two red lights in a vertical line.
(b)   Each vessel engaged in pair trawling may exhibit:
    (i)   by night, a searchlight directed forward and in the direction of the other vessel of the pair;
    (ii)   when shooting or hauling their nets or when the nets have come fast upon an obstruction, the lights prescribed in 2(a) above.

3. Signals of purse seiners

Vessels engaged in fishing with purse seine gear may exhibit two yellow lights in a vertical line. These lights shall flash alternately every second and with equal light and occultation duration. These lights may be exhibited only when the vessel is hampered by its fishing gear.

Discussion
Should you encounter a fishing fleet and be able to discern these light signals by the naked eye, you are probably far too close and the best thing you can do is to turn about and steer a reciprocal course until you can steer clear around the fleet. Remember that trawlers and purse seine gear can extent for many hundreds of feet from the boats so once again, give them a very wide berth.

124

9
ANNEX III
Technical Details
of Sound-Signal Appliances

1. Whistles

(a) *Frequencies and range of audibility*

The fundamental frequency of the signal shall lie within the range 70–700 Hz.

The range of audibility of the signal from a whistle shall be determined by those frequencies, which may include the fundamental and/or one or more higher frequencies, which lie within the range 180–700 Hz (± 1 per cent) and which provide the sound pressure levels specified in paragraph 1(c) below.

(b) *Limits of fundamental frequencies*

To ensure a wide variety of whistle characteristics, the fundamental frequency of a whistle shall be between the following limits:

(i)   70–200 Hz, for a vessel 200 metres or more in length;

(ii)   130–350 Hz, for a vessel 75 metres but less than 200 metres in length;

(iii)   250–700 Hz, for a vessel less than 75 metres in length.

(c) *Sound signal intensity and range of audibility*

A whistle fitted in a vessel shall provide, in the direction of maximum intensity of the whistle and at a distance of 1 metre from it, a sound pressure level in at least one 1/3rd octave band within the range of frequencies 180–700 Hz (± 1 per cent) of not less than the appropriate figure given in the table below.

The range of audibility in the table is for information and is approximately the range at which a whistle may be heard on its forward axis with 90 per cent probability in conditions of still air on board a vessel having average background noise level at the listening posts (takes to be 68 dB in the octave band centred on 250 Hz and 63 dB in the octave band centred on 500 Hz).

Length of vessel in metres	1/3rd-octave band level at 1 metre in dB referred to $2 \times 10^{-5} \text{ N/M}^2$	Audibility range in nautical miles
200 or more	143	2.0
75 but less than 200	138	1.5
20 but less than 75	130	1.0
Less than 20	120	0.5

In practice the range at which a whistle may be heard is extremely variable and depends critically on weather conditions; the values given can be regarded as typical but under conditions of strong wind or high ambient noise level at the listening post the range may be much reduced.

(d) *Directional properties*

The sound pressure level of a directional whistle shall be not more than 4 dB below the prescribed sound pressure level on the axis at any direction in the horizontal plane within $\pm$ 45 degrees of the axis. The sound pressure level at any other direction in the horizontal plane shall be not more than 10 dB below the prescribed sound pressure level on the axis, so that the range in any direction will be at least half the range on the forward axis. The sound pressure level shall be measured in that $\frac{1}{3}$ rd-octave band which determines the audibility range.

(e) *Positioning of whistles*

When a directional whistle is to be used as the only whistle on a vessel, it shall be installed with its maximum intensity directed straight ahead.

A whistle shall be placed as high as practicable on a vessel, in order to reduce interception of the emitted sound by obstructions and also to minimize hearing damage risk to personnel. The sound pressure level of the vessel's own signal at listening posts shall not exceed 110 dB (A) and so far as practicable should not exceed 100 dB (A).

(f) *Fitting of more than one whistle*

If whistles are fitted at a distance apart of more than 100 metres, it shall be so arranged that they are not sounded simultaneously.

(g) *Combined whistle systems*

If due to the presence of obstructions the sound field of a single whistle or one of the whistles referred to in paragraph 1(f) above is likely to have a zone of greatly reduced signal level, it is recommended that a combined whistle system be fitted so as to overcome this reduction. For the purposes of the Rules a combined whistle system is to be regarded as a single whistle. The whistles of a combined system shall be located at a distance apart of not more than 100 metres and arranged to be sounded simultaneously. The frequency of any one whistle shall differ from those of the others by at least 10 Hz.

2. Bell or gong

(a) *Intensity of signal*

A bell or gong, or other device having similar sound characteristics shall produce a sound pressure level of not less than 110 dB at a distance of 1 metre from it.

(b) *Construction*

Bells and gongs shall be made of corrosion-resistant material and designed to give a clear tone. The diameter of the mouth of the bell shall be not less than 300mm for vessels of 20 metres or more in length, and shall be not less than 200mm for vessels for 12 metres or more, but of less than 20 metres in length. Where practicable, a power-driven bell striker is recommended to ensure constant force but manual operation shall be possible. The mass of the striker shall be not less than 3 per cent of the mass of the bell.

3. Approval

The construction of sound signal appliances, their performance and their installation on board the vessels shall be to the satisfaction of the appropriate authority of the State whose flag the vessel is entitled to fly.

10
ANNEX IV

Distress Signals

1. The following signals, used or exhibited either together or separately, indicate distress and need of assistance:

(a) a gun or other explosive signal fired at intervals of about a minute;

(b) continuous sounding with any fog-signalling apparatus;

(c) rockets or shells, throwing red stars fired one at a time at short intervals;

(d) a signal made by radio-telegraphy or by any other signalling method consisting of the group $\cdots - - - \cdots$ (SOS) in the Morse code;

(e) a signal sent by radio-telephony consisting of the spoken word 'Mayday';

(f) the International Code Signal of distress indicated by N.C.;

(g) a signal consisting of a square flag having above or below it a ball or anything resembling a ball;

(h) flames on the vessel (as from a burning tar barrel, oil barrel, etc.);

(i) a rocket parachute flare or a hand-flare showing a red light;

(j) a smoke signal giving off orange-coloured smoke;

(k) slowly and repeatedly raising and lowering arms outstretched to each side;

(l) the radio-telegraph alarm signal;

(m) the radio-telephone alarm signal;

(n) signals transmitted by emergency positioning-indicating radio beacons;

(o) approved signals transmitted by radiocommunication systems.

2. The use or exhibition of any of the foregoing signals except for the purpose of indicating distress and need of assistance and the use of other signals which may be confused with any of the above signals is prohibited.

3. Attention is drawn to the relevant section of the International Code of Signals, the Merchant Ship Search and Rescue Manual and the following signals:

(a) a piece of orange-coloured canvas with either a black-square and circle or other appropriate symbol (for identification from the air);

(b) a dye marker.

These must be learnt so that they can be used when appropriate and also so that they can never be used inadvertently.

Discussion

Hopefully you will never have to use any of the above signals. By understanding and following the rules, although not necessarily slavishly, and the practice of good seamanship you should be able to avoid any dangers involving other vessels.

INDEX